What
Faith
Is Not

What
Faith
Is Not

Mitch Finley

SHEED & WARD

Franklin, Wisconsin

As an apostolate of the Priests of the Sacred Heart, a Catholic
religious congregation, the mission of Sheed & Ward is to publish books
of contemporary impact and enduring merit in Catholic Christian thought
and action. The books published, however, reflect the opinion of their
authors and are not meant to represent the official position of the
Priests of the Sacred Heart.

2001

Sheed & Ward
7373 South Lovers Lane Road
Franklin, Wisconsin 53132
1-800-266-5564

Printed in the United States of America

Cover and interior design: GrafixStudio, Inc.

Scripture quotations are from the New Revised Standard Version of the
Bible, copyright 1946, 1952, 1971 by the Division of Christian Education
of the National Council of the Churches of Christ in the USA. Used by
permission. All rights reserved.

Library of Congress Cataloging-in-Publication Data

Finley, Mitch.
    What faith is not / Mitch Finley.
        p. cm.
    ISBN 1-58051-103-1
    1. Faith. 2. Christian life—Catholic authors. I. Title

 BV4637 .F445 2001
 234'.23--dc21   2001041128

1 2 3 4 5 / 04 03 02 01

Contents

Introduction

Why a book on what faith is not?

Religious language has a specific purpose—to make it possible for people to talk about human religious experience. In particular, for Christians religious language exists so we can talk about God, Jesus, the Holy Spirit, and the central mysteries of the Christian faith. The trouble is that language is tied to human ideas, and these ideas are necessarily limited in nature. It simply is not possible for finite human concepts to fully express the infinite.

On the one hand, human language is all we have to speak of God, and human language does indeed carry true and accurate knowledge about God and about human experience of God. On the other hand, because human ideas are finite, this means that religious language can also mislead. In other words, religious language can both reveal and conceal.

The *Catechism of the Catholic Church* puts it this way:

> Since our knowledge of God is limited, our language about him is equally so. We can name God only by taking creatures as our starting point, and in accordance with our limited human ways of knowing and thinking.[1]

To repeat, religious language both reveals and conceals. It's all we have to talk about God and religious experience, but we need to keep in mind that it is easy for religious language to mislead as well as lead. Also, over time—centuries, in fact—religious language has a tendency to become distorted. Even so basic a word as *God* takes on countless shades of meaning and its nuances become almost endless. *God* can easily mean something different to one person than to another person.

Depending on all kinds of factors and influences, *God* may evoke strong feelings of fear and guilt, even anger, for one person, feelings of security, love, and trust in another person, and emotional indifference in a third person. So much depends on how parents, teachers, and other significant adults use the word *God* during the years when we are children.

For many people one of the most important—and sometimes difficult—tasks of adulthood is to purify their religious language. Often, adults need to bring their religious concepts into line with the truth of what these concepts are meant to refer to. Sometimes adults need to do some work to dissociate religious language from inappropriate feelings and ideas. This is one of the tasks of an adult religion and an adult spirituality.

Take another conventional word for example, this time *salvation*. Ask a Christian fundamentalist what this word means, and you are likely to hear that salvation means being "saved" from your sins and rescued from eternity in hell. A fundamentalist is likely to quote for you from various scriptural texts, such as the familiar parable of the sheep and the goats in Matthew 25:

> "Then [the king, i.e. God] will say to those at his left hand,
> 'You that are accursed, depart from me into the eternal fire
> prepared for the devil and his angels . . .'" (41)

A fundamentalist Christian will tell you that *salvation* requires that you "accept Jesus Christ as your personal savior." Only in this way can you avoid going to hell when you die.

In fact, it is not only fundamentalist Christians who recite a formula about being saved from hell when asked about *salvation*. This is a fairly standard understanding among most Christians, even those who do not believe that *salvation* can happen the second you "accept

Jesus Christ as your personal savior." The most common understanding of *salvation* is that after death you will avoid hell and gain heaven.

A closer look at New Testament scholarship since the mid-twentieth century offers a more nuanced understanding of *salvation*. In the New Testament, *salvation* means "liberation from bondage to sin and death."[2] This understanding steps away from a literalist vision of being rescued from the flames of hell following death, on the one hand; and, on the other hand, it allows *salvation* to become a concept that encompasses this life and this world, as well as the next life and one's destiny after death.

We might say that *salvation* is about healing and liberation in both this life and the next. This is an understanding that is likely to make more sense to people of the twenty-first century than an understanding that limits itself to a literalist mythology of escape from a literal eternity in the literal fires of hell that has little to do with here and now.

The point is, of course, that *salvation*, too, is a religious word that, among a random selection of a dozen people, you will not find a shared understanding. Even if all twelve people identify themselves as Christians, you are likely to find a lack of agreement about the meaning of this word. Should you sprinkle into the mix a few Jews, a couple of Muslims, two or three Buddhists and Hindus, and the occasional Unitarian, you will find even less of a consensus.

Pause and think of all the conventional religious terms about which you could conduct a similar discussion: *sin, grace, repentance, church, redemption, God* . . . and, of course, *faith*, which is what this book is all about. *Faith* is one of the most common of religious terms, but it is also one of the most frequently misunderstood. Each chapter in this book will take a common misunderstanding of *faith* and examine it in some detail. The purpose of each reflection is to better understand what faith is *not* in order to come to a better understanding of what faith truly is.

Some words of Thomas Merton (1915–1968), the great twentieth-century Trappist monk, poet, author, and social critic, as well as a convert to Catholicism, are relevant. Commenting late in his life on his Catholic faith, Merton wrote in his journal:

> There is nothing more important than the gift of Catholic Faith—and keeping that faith pure and clear."[3]

The purpose of our reflections in this book, whether you are Christian or of some other persuasion, is to nourish your ongoing effort to keep your faith "pure and clear"; to rid your faith of mistaken, distorted, or unbalanced notions so that your faith can be stronger and more vibrant; so it can shine out more clearly in this world and be a brighter witness to the One from whom faith comes as a gift.

At the same time, I want to make it clear that, as the author of this book, I don't claim to have a complete grasp of all truth. I am as much of a searcher as you are, reader. I speak simply as one who has given this topic some thought, and I would like to share what I have come up with. Together perhaps we can get a little closer to the truth of what faith is all about.

1

Faith is not a spiritual aspirin

Sometimes both believers and unbelievers have the notion that faith is supposed to be some kind of painkiller, spiritual aspirin, or ibuprofen, or acetaminophen that will, if not eliminate life's anguish and hurts, at least dull the pain. Sometimes believers think that if they suffer when life is a pain, then that means that their faith is weak or nonexistent. Sometimes unbelievers accuse religious people of being weak-spined, saying that religion is little more than a way to inoculate yourself against what Shakespeare's *Hamlet* called "the slings and arrows of outrageous fortune."[1]

Such believers and unbelievers are wrong, of course. Faith is not, and can never be, a spiritual painkiller. When life becomes a headache, or a pain in the derrière or the heart, faith helps you to face up to it, not run the other direction. Sometimes we may forget that even though he was the Son of God, because he was also fully human during his earthly life Jesus had to have faith. Because he was divine he had a unique ontological intimacy with his Father—that is, an intimacy that existed on the most basic level of his being; because he was human, he was a man of prayer. Therefore, Jesus is the ultimate model of faith.

For Jesus, faith was no painkiller. The Gospels make a point of showing us, in fact, that the faith of Jesus compelled him to accept pain and suffering, not run away from it. In the Gospels we find a Jesus for whom faith was anything but a dose of morphine. The following lines from the Gospels do not show us a Jesus whose faith was a painkiller:

> They went to a place called Gethsemane; and [Jesus] said to his disciples, "Sit here while I pray." He took with him Peter and James and John, and began to be distressed and agitated. And he said to them, "I am deeply grieved, even to death; remain here, and keep awake." And going a little farther, he threw himself on the ground and prayed that, if it were possible, the hour might pass from him. He said, "Abba, Father, for you all things are possible; remove this cup from me; yet, not what I want, but what you want" (Mark 14:32–36).

〜

> He took with him Peter and the two sons of Zebedee, and began to be grieved and agitated. Then he said to them, "I am deeply grieved, even to death; remain here, and stay awake with me." And going a little farther, he threw himself on the ground and prayed, "My Father, if it is possible, let this cup pass from me; yet not what I want but what you want" (Matthew 26:37–39).

〜

> In his anguish he prayed more earnestly, and his sweat became like great drops of blood falling down on the ground (Luke 22:44).

The faith of Jesus did not save him from pain and suffering, neither during his lifetime nor as he hung dying on the cross. So it would be completely inappropriate for us to think of faith as a way to escape pain and suffering, a kind of spiritual Novocain. Neither, however, does faith result in a psychologically ill person who seeks out pain and suffering, who "enjoys" pain. A person of faith is no masochist. It's clear from the gospel passages quoted above that Jesus did not *want* to suffer; yet for him the bottom line was to accept the mystery of his Father's will. If pain and suffering were unavoidable, he was ready to accept them, and that is what faith does: it accepts pain and suffering, when they are unavoidable, for the sake of the greater mystery of God's will in one's life.

This raises another big question, however. Does God want us to experience pain and suffering? Did he want Jesus to suffer? Does he want us to suffer? Is our God a sadist who enjoyed watching his own Son suffer and die? Does he enjoy watching us suffer and, ultimately, die? So here we are in the middle of one of the great mysteries of human existence: the mystery of suffering and death.

To call suffering a mystery, however, does not mean we can sidestep the need to try to understand it better. Yes, human suffering is a mystery, and it is a mystery in which Christian faith finds itself united to the suffering, death—and Resurrection!—of Jesus. Yes, in the final analysis we can only accept the great mystery of suffering in faith. But after all that, we are still left with the question "*Why?*" Why must we suffer at all? Perhaps the best, though still woefully inadequate, answer is one that is scandalously philosophical—"scandalously," because this answer can seem to be indifferent to the reality of the pain and anguish of real, felt human suffering. Still, it may be the best we can do.

Perhaps there is suffering precisely because we human beings are a blend, in our own selves, of the physical and the spiritual. We are embodied souls, or soul-filled bodies, and our inherent dynamic, or orientation, is toward a perfect unity of soul and body, and as we move toward this unity in space and time, one unavoidable consequence is suffering on various levels of our being. We have physical, emotional, psychological, and spiritual suffering, and they are all, finally, a result of movement toward our ultimate destiny: perfect body-soul unity beyond space and time. Suffering is a result of our imperfect condition, and it has nothing to do with personal faults or personal guilt. Suffering simply *is*.

Just as a woman suffers when giving birth to a baby, so we suffer as we give birth to ourselves. Faith, authentic Christian faith, sheds light on our suffering by showing us that in our suffering we are with and in Christ, who embraced human suffering as well. In other words, the only way to make any sense at all out of suffering is by means of a Christian mysticism of suffering. We don't like suffering, but faith shows us that in suffering we are one with Christ who is with us in the mystery of our suffering.[2]

Note, however, that when we call human pain and suffering a "mystery," this is not merely a way to avoid trying to explain or understand it. Rather, we use the term mystery in its theological sense, as a human reality that reveals or brings us into contact with God's saving love, a love that so far transcends our ability to understand it that we can never hope to do so. Instead of comprehending the mystery of pain and suffering, we are "comprehended by" it; through pain and suffering we are grasped by God's love in a way we simply cannot fathom. "It is not the human mind that grasps God; the divine majesty grasps us."[3]

Harsh though it may seem, we need to see that in his suffering and death Jesus was held by God's love, and the same is true for us. In a way that reveals God's love to us, it is the example of Jesus that makes unacceptable pain and suffering acceptable. For he did not refuse to accept this mysterious part of being human but embraced it even to the point of the worst kind of suffering and death. In other words, Jesus went there so the person of faith finds it possible to go there, too. If ever the term "blind trust" has meaning, it is in the midst of pain and suffering that this happens.

Our God takes no pleasure in the pain and suffering of his Son or in the pain and suffering of any of his creatures, us included. We can even say that God suffers when we suffer; that God weeps when we weep; that God does not will human suffering but is with us in the midst of pain and suffering. If the image of the Son of God dying on the cross means anything, it means that he is with us in our pain, suffering, and death. It means that for a reason we cannot understand, and in a way that we cannot grasp but can experience, the pain and suffering that are unavoidable in this life are part of the process we move through from time into eternity and from death to resurrection.

We might think of a woman in labor giving birth to a child as a metaphor, only here what we're talking about is giving birth to *oneself.* It's as if the transition from time to eternity—which is much of what life is all about—is a kind of labor process, giving birth to yourself, and that transition from life to eternal life, from embodied spirit to "resurrected" embodied spirit, cannot happen apart from what we perceive as human pain and suffering. Only faith gives us the knowledge that this is so, and only faith makes it possible to experience this as so.

Far from being a form of spiritual Novocain, faith accepts unavoidable anguish, anxiety, and physical pain—while taking advantage of whatever medical relief may be available short of the evil of assisted suicide—and finds in that acceptance a mysterious, mystical union with the suffering, death, and Resurrection of Christ. There comes a point where words simply no longer serve, and only those who know great pain and suffering have the right to talk about the intimacy between faith and human suffering.

Catholicism often holds up saints as examples of heroic suffering, and sometimes stories about saints seem to present an acceptance of suffering that seems to border on masochism. Take St. Thérèse of Lisieux, the author of *Story of a Soul,* one of the most popular spiritual classics of our era.[4] This young French Carmelite nun died of tuberculosis at the age of twenty-four in 1897. The afternoon of her death it seemed that her agony would never end. Thérèse said, "Am I not to die yet? Very well, let it be so. I do not wish to suffer less."[5]

The point was not that Thérèse wanted to suffer. The point was that she accepted the mystery of God's will whatever it might be, and since her suffering was unavoidable, she could only understand it as a manifestation of God's will. Had she miraculously recovered, Thérèse would have been just as willing to go along with that as to die. It was all the same to her, as long as she could unite her will with God's evident will, whatever it might be.

Theologian and storyteller John Shea recounts an event that illustrates in a humorous manner how genuine faith can be anything but a spiritual aspirin. Lying on the beach on a summer's day, Shea looked up as two young men clad in dark suits and neckties approached, carrying Bibles. One of the young men said to Shea, "Have you met Jesus Christ?" Shea replied, "Unfortunately, yes!"[6]

The two young men were not, most likely, expecting this response. But Shea's point is well taken. Sometimes to "meet Jesus Christ" can cause considerable trouble and inconvenience. Sometimes faith leads you in directions you would not choose for yourself. Authentic faith often results in taking risks, sometimes big ones. There are plenty of examples of this in the lives of saints and other extraordinarily holy men and women, of course. But there are even more examples of such a faith in the lives of ordinary men and women.

Young couples who marry with a sense that their marriage is the way they are called to live their faith take a definite risk in doing so. There are no guarantees. To conceive and give birth to children is a risk, too. Again, there are no guarantees. Parents of babies and young children sometimes think that if they do "all the right things," their children will become ideal young adults in every way. On the contrary, children have a way of being and becoming their own persons, regardless of how hard their parents try to shape them into the persons they would like them to be. It takes a faith that knows plenty of anguish to accept all this and keep on praying for one's offspring no matter what choices, for good or for ill, they may make.

The suffering that faith accepts is not limited to physical pain and suffering, of course. Sometimes to live by faith brings mental anguish and emotional insecurity—just the opposite of being a spiritual pain reliever. There are countless true stories of faith-filled people whose lives would have been far easier had they taken a pass on living the gospel. Think, for example, of the many peace activists in the late twentieth century who found themselves doing time in jail because their faith led them to take actions, technically illegal, against the proliferation of weapons of mass destruction or to protest and end the war in Vietnam.

Think of the many Christian civil rights activists during the 1950s and '60s—a Baptist minister, the Rev. Martin Luther King, Jr., the most prominent—who stuck their necks out to further the cause of African American civil rights in the United States. That they took such actions can in many cases be attributed directly to their Christian faith. For peace and civil rights activists, faith is anything but a spiritual pain reliever; just the opposite.

These are examples of situations that, while historically significant, are also extraordinary in the sense that they do not involve people living their faith in ordinary, everyday ways. To see how faith is anything but a spiritual aspirin for a faith lived in ways common to countless people of whom history takes little or no notice, we must consult our own experience and that of our relatives, friends, and acquaintances. This, after all, is how faith is lived most of the time—in unremarkable, unnoticed, yet quietly heroic ways.

Start by thinking about the experience of any married couple you know for whom faith is foundational to their marriage—not just a Sunday go-to-Mass or occasional Sunday go-to-Mass kind of faith, but a faith that defines who they are as individuals and as a couple. In some cases, this faith has been basic to a couple's marriage since they first met because it was basic for each of them before they met. In other cases, faith became central later in the couple's relationship, either after they met or maybe even later, after they had been married for some years. Regardless, the point is that for such a married couple their faith is what makes them "tick" as a couple. It's what makes it possible for them to have a successful marriage, a faithful marriage through all the ups and downs of married life and life in general. Trite as it sounds, a roller-coaster ride is sometimes a better metaphor to understand marriage than a cruise along a pleasant country highway.

Years ago, Joan Meyer Anzia, M.D., and Mary G. Durkin, D.Mn., suggested that any marriage that is alive is at some point in a constant process that is both cyclic and a spiral.[7] At any give moment in the marriage, the couple is in one of the following phases: falling in love, settling down, bottoming out, or beginning again.

Falling in love is an ecstatic, almost mystical experience, vitally important to the relationship though frequently dismissed as superficial and insignificant. Falling in love is a foretaste of heaven, and any husband and wife worth their salt will value this experience and not let it get away completely, no matter how long they are married. Falling in love, in a mature sense, should remain part of a mature, healthy marriage.

Settling down happens naturally. No couple can maintain the ecstasy of falling in love indefinitely. If they tried to do this, something in the relationship would "short circuit" and the marriage would blow a fuse. Everyday life and its requirements inevitably impinge and demand attention. Work and everything needed to maintain a domestic life bring the couple out of the mystical "high" that characterizes falling in love. The challenge is to keep the settling down phase from becoming mere boredom with each other.

Bottoming out almost invariably happens to any married couple, however. Sooner or later, husband and wife see each other's "dark side." Sooner or later, the honeymoon is over and each spouse sees the other as he or she really is, warts and all. He makes irritating noises when he eats and leaves his dirty socks lying on the bedroom floor, plus most of the time he isn't the most romantic person in the world. She sheds tears for what seems like no reason, squeezes the toothpaste tube in the middle, and stays in the shower using up the hot water for way too long. He likes to stay up late most nights. She likes to go to bed early. He enjoys watching football for hours on weekends. She wants to go for long bicycle rides on weekends. In-laws interfere. Children are a joy, but they are also, at tmes, a source of great stress. Sometimes addictions surface for one or both spouses. Eventually, it all adds up, and the marriage feels boring, irritating, on the skids, or on the rocks.

Beginning again is always an option, however, as this is where faith is particularly important in a marriage, and it's a faith that is no fun, for sure, no painkiller, no spiritual Novocain. It's a faith that has a distinctive marital character, however, in that it is sexual. Anzia and Durkin described it thus:

> There is a powerful, sexual, unreasonable feeling between us that we cannot destroy; it seems to be given. It is so incongruous, it is almost funny. We are under the spell of a very mysterious turn of events when we least expect it. The rediscovery of our sexual passion in "the pits" of our life together is a graced moment.[8]

When a marriage bottoms out, whether the dominant emotion in that experience is anger or boredom, or some mix of the two, faith gives the grace to begin again—if husband and wife are open to that faith. It's a faith that requires each one to die to self, to let go of righteous anger or the false security of boredom, and give in to, of all things, sexual passion. It takes faith to do this, a faith that is like iron and may seem just as cold at the time.

The most common experience of a faith that is no pain reliever is that shared by parents, regardless of the ages of their children. From the moment a baby is born, that child normally is a source of deep joy to parents. But there is no getting around the fact that children can be, and often are, a source of much anguish, worry, irritation, stress, and disappointment. It's the rare parent who has ideal children, kids who excel, never get in trouble, and meet all parental expectations.

The tendency of a consumer culture to romanticize children and parenthood in order to sell commodities contributes to parental guilt when children don't measure up to the romantic ideal—when the baby doesn't behave like the babies in the television commercials or look like the baby on the baby-food-jar label; when the two- or three-year-old pitches a fit in the supermarket; when the eight-year-old acts out in school or shows no interest in getting good grades; when the preteen decides to try cigarettes or marijuana; when the teenager needs medication for depression or wrecks the car.

Parents who bring a living faith to their role know that this faith is anything but a painkiller. Considerable mental pain, emotional anguish, and many sleepless nights come with trying to be a good parent for your kids and, at the same time, entrust them to God's love. Faith does not and never will mean that children will not do the wrong thing and suffer the consequences. Faith does not mean that God will intervene to make sure that your kids do not make stupid choices. Faith does not mean that you ask God to take care of it, after which you magically get a good, full-night's sleep. For parents, faith is more a leap into the void without a parachute than a warm blanket or a side-effects-free sleeping pill.

Rather than being a painkiller, faith, for parents, is like an inflated inner tube. You still find yourself immersed in an ocean of uncertainty and darkness, but because of faith you don't sink completely. You keep your head above water. You hang on; you don't let go. You manage to make it through the humiliation of meeting with the counselor with your teenager after he or she was caught in school with marijuana in his or her backpack. You keep your self-respect intact after your daughter or son is expelled from school for doing something as stupid as the day is long. And so forth.

Faith, for parents, does not numb the pain. But it does help you to maintain some perspective, to keep your eyes on the future, on the fact that your child has a future, that this present moment of darkness is not the last word. He or she will grow up, will more than likely become a mature person who makes better choices in life. In other words, the faith of parents gives them *hope*, but it does not take away the anguish or nights of lost sleep; it does not take away the cross.

Marriage and parenthood are ways we experience the cross and Resurrection of Christ, and the same may be said of any way that we go about living our faith, any vocation to which we are called. The experience of having your parents divorce is a source of suffering, too, and a genuine experience of the cross. Many young people today can relate to this, and many ask why they had to go through this pain when they had nothing to do with causing it. Faith replies that there is, in the end, no way to understand it. All you can do is see in this experience the cross of Christ, and when you do the best you can with it, you'll find yourself on the receiving end of the healing that can only come from his Resurrection.

Each of these experiences, and countless others, is a way to live our faith, each is a way to follow the way of the cross and rejoice in the Resurrection—and the two can never be separated. No cross, no resurrection—in a way not intended by the original meaning of the slogan, "no pain, no gain." Regardless of the way of life we end up living, whatever it is, it's the way we are called to live our faith, and that means it's our particular way of the cross and our particular path to resurrection.

If we expect faith to save us from the dark side of life, we are in for a big disappointment, and this should come as no surprise. If we whine when life becomes a pain in the backside, we might be well advised to return to the Gospels to regain our focus. We would be well advised to reread passages such as:

> Then Jesus told his disciples, "If any want to become my followers, let them deny themselves and take up their cross and follow me. For those who want to save their life will lose it, and those who lose their life for my sake will find it" (Matthew 16:24–25).

We don't like to hear this; or at least we don't like to accept the truth of such words. We resist the idea that to follow Christ in this world means, inevitably, not only to encounter pain and suffering but to not be surprised by it, not feel sorry for ourselves about it, and live with it without whining about it. This is what faith is supposed to do: help us not be surprised by pain and suffering, not indulge in self-pity, and not whine about it. Pain and suffering, disappointment and disillusionment, are part of the human condition, part of the package. Faith does not make the darkness go away; rather, it helps us live with it and act like a grown-up about it. Faith helps us live with it and not despair, live with it and not whine about it.

No discussion of the role of faith in the face of pain and suffering can afford to neglect the story of Job in the Hebrew Scriptures, or the Old Testament. The Book of Job is a divinely inspired novella and one of the greatest works of fiction ever written. The tale begins with an encounter between God and Satan:

> One day the heavenly beings came to present themselves before the LORD, and Satan also came among them. The LORD said to Satan, "Where have you come from?" Satan answered the LORD, "From going to and fro on the earth, and from walking up and down on it."
>
> The LORD said to Satan, "Have you considered my servant Job? There is no one like him on the earth, a blameless and upright man who fears God and turns away from evil."
>
> Then Satan answered the LORD, "Does Job fear God for nothing? Have you not put a fence around him and his house and all that he has, on every side? You have blessed the work of his hands, and his possessions have increased in the land. But stretch out your hand now, and touch all that he has, and he will curse you to your face."
>
> The LORD said to Satan, "Very well, all that he has is in your power; only do not stretch out your hand against him!"
>
> So Satan went out from the presence of the LORD (1:6–12).

Notice that God *allows* Satan to cause pain and suffering for Job, God does not cause pain and suffering himself—an important distinction for the Book of Job. Satan brings grief upon Job, a good and innocent man. Job does not respond with anger toward God, however. He simply says that God gave and God can take away. Still, Job has his questions, and he feels that he has a right to ask them. However, friends of Job—Eliphaz the Temanite, Bildad the Shuhite, and Zophar the Naamathite, plus the youthful Elihu—berate him for questioning God and insist that Job deserves what he is getting. But Job refuses to give up his questions; he wants to know why he should suffer so. Finally, God replies by asking Job who he thinks he is:

> "Where were you when I laid the foundation of the earth? Tell me, if you have understanding. Who determined its measurements—surely you know! Or who stretched the line upon it? On what were its bases sunk, or who laid its cornerstone when the morning stars sang together and all the heavenly beings shouted for joy?

"Or who shut in the sea with doors when it burst out from the womb?—when I made the clouds its garment, and thick darkness its swaddling band, and prescribed bounds for it, and set bars and doors, and said, 'Thus far shall you come, and no farther, and here shall your proud waves be stopped'?

"Have you commanded the morning since your days began, and caused the dawn to know its place, so that it might take hold of the skirts of the earth, and the wicked be shaken out of it?" (38:4–13)

For the Book of Job, the idea that faith should be a relief from pain and suffering is absurd, because no human can possibly understand how pain and suffering fit into the overwhelming mystery of God's will and ways. While later philosophers became more sophisticated at questioning how an all-good and all-merciful God could allow innocent children to suffer and die, the response of the Book of Job still stands.

The mistaken notion that faith should be spiritual aspirin to relieve the spiritual and emotional aches and pains of daily life, and/or a dose of spiritual morphine when pain and suffering are great, depends for its survival on the assumption that pain and suffering are *ultimately* meaningless. But this is where Christian faith, in particular, insists that there is no way we can know that this is so. In fact, because the Son of God drank from the cup of human suffering, to the last drop, we must insist on the contrary, even if we cannot fully explain it. For wherever we go, the Son of God and son of Mary—fully human and fully divine—is there waiting for us, which means that even pain and suffering is a place of union with him.

We must also acknowledge, however, that the mystery of God and the mystery of human existence includes far more than suffering. We need to keep at arm's length a tendency to have a "the-glass-is-half-empty" outlook on life. Rather, the mystery of all things includes the great and wonderful mystery that so much joy and goodness is a part of the picture. Instead of asking, "How can there be suffering?" we might just as well ask, "How can there be joy?" Both questions are justifiable, after all. We live in the midst of the great mystery of being human and being alive, and this great mystery is a great blend of joy and sorrow. Ultimately, perhaps, it comes down to which we think is greater, and which is the key to "What It's All About?" For Christian faith, joy is final while suffering is not.

Finally, the witness of countless Christians down through the centuries, and the witness of many saints, reminds us that when we suffer, our pain can become a prayer. We can offer our unavoidable sufferings, great and small, in union with the suffering of Christ as a form of prayer for the benefit of others. Faith does not seek suffering, but it does accept it as a part of the great mystery of human existence in union with the death and Resurrection of Christ. Faith does you the great favor of giving you something with which to respond to the fact of pain and suffering. Instead of facing suffering with helpless despair, faith gives you something to respond with, the conviction that suffering is never, ultimately, meaningless.

The great mid-twentieth century Catholic fiction writer Flannery O'Connor said it as well as any, and better than most. In a letter she wrote in 1959, O'Connor said:

> What people don't realize is how much religion costs. They think faith is a big electric blanket, when of course it is the cross. It is much harder to believe than not to believe.[9]

Faith is not a source of secret knowledge

In the early centuries of Christianity, a system of religious belief developed that scholars in modern times labeled "Gnosticism." This name comes from the Greek word *gnosis,* which means "knowledge." Gnostics believed that salvation depended upon having a particular knowledge or inner enlightenment that would free a person from the evil and ignorance of life in this world.

No one is sure exactly where and when Gnosticism originated, but we do know that it was influential during the early decades of Christianity and included some anti-Christian doctrines. Gnostic teachers denied, for example, Jesus' full humanity and refused to accept both the Old and New Testaments. Gnosticism also denied the teaching authority of the Church and Christian tradition.

Mainly because much of what we know about it comes to us second hand from early Christian anti-Gnostic writings, it is difficult to understand Gnosticism completely, but we do know that it was dualistic: it taught that the human soul is imprisoned in the body and in creation as a whole, and that creation is controlled by evil forces. In particular, Gnosticism taught that all of creation is in the control of a semi-divine being called the "demiurge." At the same time,

Gnosticism taught that humans have a desire for goodness and truth that exist outside the created order.

Gnosticism also taught that there is a completely transcendent God—totally outside of space and time—who sent a bearer of divine knowledge and enlightenment into the evil created world. Gnostics held that people who accept this secret knowledge (*gnosis*) can be helped to escape from the evil-created order into the spiritual realm of truth and goodness.

Those who embraced Gnosticism believed that they were saved by the divine enlightenment they had received, while everyone else would spend eternity in hell for their choice to continue living in ignorance. Finally, Gnosticism was also a blend of elements from various religious and philosophical systems of thought. It included ideas and beliefs from Greek mystery cults, Jewish mysticism, Iranian dualism, Babylonian and Egyptian myths, and Christian Scriptures and rituals.[1]

Now, the point of all this is that the Christian religion is not a form of Gnosticism. Christian faith is not a source of some esoteric, secret knowledge about divine things completely unavailable to anyone else. People of faith do not have exact "inside information" about anything. Faith does not give a person secret knowledge of God's will. Catholicism insists that it is perfectly possible—in fact, it happens all the time—for people to come to a knowledge of God's existence and self-revelation by their inborn powers alone. For example, the whole natural world and created order are, in themselves, a revelation of God and of God's nature—a "book," as it were, that is open to all prior to and even apart from any exposure to explicitly Christian revelation. In his Letter to the Romans, St. Paul even faults those who refuse to make use of this inborn ability:

> For the wrath of God is revealed from heaven against all ungodliness and wickedness of those who by their wicked-ness suppress the truth. For what can be known about God is plain to them, because God has shown it to them. Ever since the creation of the world his eternal power and divine nature, invisible though they are, have been understood and seen through the things he has made. So they are with-out excuse; for though they knew God, they did not honor him as God or give thanks to him, but they became futile in their thinking, and their senseless minds were darkened (1:18–21).

The Catholic Church teaches that it is of God's nature, as it were, to reveal himself to us. As the *Catechism* states:

> God, infinitely perfect and blessed in himself, in a plan of sheer goodness freely created man to make him share in his own blessed life. For this reason, at every time and in every place, God draws close to man (n. 2).

At the same time, Catholicism also teaches that apart from God's grace, natural human powers can only go so far in coming to know God. There comes a point where further human knowledge of God becomes impossible apart from God's self-revelation in the Judeo-Christian tradition. Does this mean, then, that there is a way in which faith *does* give knowledge about divine realities and divine truths unavailable in any other way? Yes, but not in the way that Gnosticism taught. Rather, faith gives a *finite* knowledge about divine realities because it is not possible for humans to completely grasp the Infinite. It is more accurate to say that in faith you are *grasped by* God.

We gain knowledge of divine realities, but not because we fully comprehend truths that are eternal. Rather, the "knowledge" we gain comes from being *grasped by* God. We gain knowledge of God in the way that a drop of rain falling into the ocean gains "knowledge" of the ocean. Our "knowledge" is more experiential than cognitive.

Of course, there is a secondary sense in which we gain knowledge as a result of faith. Because we are encompassed by God's love, because his love dwells in us and enlightens our mind, that makes it possible for us to receive the Scriptures, and the word of God that they communicate, with an understanding not available to the person without faith who reads the Scriptures merely as "literature." In a similar but lesser sense, the person of faith can receive official church documents, such as the *Catechism of the Catholic Church*, or documents issued by church councils, as more than just the opinions of a committee. In this sense, then, faith makes it possible to have "information" about divine realities that the person without faith does not have.

The knowledge that comes from faith, however, is a knowledge that fulfills and completes knowledge about divine realities available to anyone, as discussed above. Without faith, a person can become aware of a benevolent God who created all things. This is a knowledge of divine realities available to all. With faith, however, a person can come to a deeper understanding of this God and learn far more about him than the person without faith.

Lest we slip into semi-Gnosticism, however, it is important to keep in mind that we are still not talking about a form of secret knowledge, some set of esoteric ideas, or propositions, or teachings, that one must understand and accept in order to be "saved." The "knowledge" that comes from faith might best be compared to the "knowledge" that close friends have of one another as a consequence of their friendship. Even better, the "knowledge" that faith gives is like the "knowledge" husband and wife have of each other in a loving marriage.

You "know" your good friend, or you "know" your spouse, because you have a *relationship* with each other. Especially in a marriage, you have a *commitment* to each other, one that keeps you in touch with each other not just on the surface but in your hearts and for "the long haul." Husband and wife know each other intimately, from the inside out and from the outside in. Consequently, they have a "knowledge" of each other that others do not have. The "knowledge" that comes from faith is something like this.

Faith comes first of all from a personal encounter between God and the person in the context of a community that has an ongoing relationship with him that goes back, back, for many, many centuries. You encounter God in the context of this faith community and its history and sacred tradition, and the result of this personal encounter is what we call "faith." In turn, this faith brings a kind of "knowledge" comparable to the "knowledge" that husband and wife have of each other in a loving marriage.

Because of your ongoing personal encounter with God in the context of the faith community's ongoing personal history with this God, you have both a personal knowledge of God and you share in the community's collective knowledge of God gathered over many centuries. There is nothing secret about this knowledge, but it does become available only to those who allow themselves to be embraced by God's love in the context of this particular community of faith.

At the same time, it is important to know that faith does not bring with it some special knowledge that gives Christians an advantage in the everyday world over nonreligious people or those who belong to other religious traditions. Faith does not make you better equipped to become economically successful, for example, or more politically adept, or more likely to have children who are bright and successful in the eyes of the world.

The knowledge that faith gives is not knowledge *about* anything. Rather, it is knowledge *of* God and of God's personal presence as the incomprehensible Divine Mystery at the heart of the universe who dwells in the world, in all people, and in you, in love. If anything, faith-knowing will make you *less* concerned about worldly success, power, and prestige than the kinds of knowledge that make the world go around.

Young people who, after college, spend a couple of years with the Jesuit Volunteer Corps, often say, with a smile, that their experience in JVC "ruined me for life." By this they mean that the kind of faith experience they have for those two years, living in community, serving others for almost no pay at all, makes them unbelievers in a culture that celebrates wealth, power, prestige, and superficial appearances. These young people often gain a knowledge of God and the deeper dimensions of human existence that leaves them with no desire to earn their first million dollars before they are thirty.

Microsoft founder Bill Gates's charitable giving is almost beyond belief. The man gives away literally billions of dollars annually to good causes of various sorts. At the same time, Bill Gates was once quoted as saying that he thinks there are more useful ways to spend an hour on Sunday morning than sitting in church. This is the kind of remark you would expect the wealthiest man in the world to make, to the point that Gates practically offers himself as a mere stereotype of the fabulously wealthy but spiritually shallow person. Bill Gates didn't accumulate his billions of dollars by being stupid, but his knowledge seems to be mostly of the kind that makes the world go around. He does not present himself to the world as a man of faith but as a man of practical know-how and technical expertise.

Would it not be possible for someone to be a person of authentic faith and also become fabulously wealthy? Perhaps, but don't hold your breath. Faith and a desire to work, and work, and work to become successful and rich don't often come together in the same person. Something about the gospel tends to make people want to move in the other direction, toward accumulating less, not more; toward simplicity of life rather than the lifestyles of the rich and famous. The knowledge that comes with faith is a knowledge that, as Jesus declares matter-of-factly in the Gospel of Mark, "It is easier for a camel to go through the eye of a needle than for someone who is rich to enter the kingdom of God" (10:25). Such knowledge tends to make you a poor candidate to become the next Bill Gates.

It is far more common for someone to become wealthy, or inherit wealth, and then begin to ask deeper questions. Sometimes wealthy people experience a religious conversion of some sort and then struggle to manage their wealth in ways consistent with an authentic faith. Sometimes this involves a major shift in lifestyle, sometimes not so noticeable a shift. Regardless, it is quite possible to be wealthy and find yourself with the knowledge that faith gives, then begin to act on that knowledge in ways that put your wealth at the service of love of God and neighbor. Examples of this are too numerous to count. Still, it would probably be accurate to say that more people who become or find themselves wealthy do not go through such a personal transformation than those who do. Wealth can be a kind of addiction and one not easy to kick.

The knowledge that comes from faith takes many forms, but it is so simple that in the minds of many people it has been reduced to being almost trite. Far from being a secret, the knowledge that comes from faith is common coin. It can easily be fit into a nutshell, but when you understand it you see that it encompasses everything from the vast and starry universe to the tiniest molecule; everything from relations between the nations of the world to the deepest intimacy between two individual persons. The knowledge that comes from faith has many formulations, depending on everything from historical circumstances to personal points of view.

The knowledge that faith gives percolates in the heart of each person of faith, and each one may express it in different ways at different times, in different places. Each reveals, but each also conceals. Each is true as far as it goes, but each one goes only so far, and there is always more to be said. Here are just a few of the ways that people of faith down through the centuries expressed the knowledge that faith gives:

"All shall be well, and all shall be well, and all manner of thing shall be well."

Blessed Julian of Norwich (c. 1342–1423)

⌇

"Every day is a messenger of God."

Russian proverb

⌇

"Most of the trouble in the world is caused by people wanting to be important."

T. S. Eliot (1888–1965)

⌇

"Take away love and our earth is a tomb."

Robert Browning (1812–1889)

⌇

"You need not cry very loud; [God] is closer to us than we think."

Brother Lawrence (1611–1691)

⌇

"If we go down into ourselves we find that we possess exactly what we desire."

Simone Weil (1909–1943)

⌇

"God is full of compassion, and never fails those who are afflicted and despised, if they trust in him alone."

Saint Teresa of Avila (1515–1582)

⌇

"I was a nonbeliever until the day it dawned on me that the absolute voice of nothingness in which I could not possibly see anything or hear anything was also the absolute fullness of everything. . ."

Thomas Merton (1915–1968)

∽

All expressions of the knowledge that faith gives say the same thing, and they all say something different. But they all come from experience of the same revealing mystery, which is faith—even in the case of someone like the mid-twentieth century French seeker Simone Weil, who never formally became a Christian. Jewish by birth, she became highly educated and spent her young adulthood searching for truth and God. When she died from tuberculosis in 1943, at the age of thirty-four, she had decided that although the Catholic Church had the truth, she did not yet have the gift of faith.

At the risk of seeming to be needlessly obscure, there is a very real sense in which the knowledge that comes from faith, as Thomas Merton suggested, is the knowledge that "the absolute voice of nothingness" is also "the absolute fullness of everything." This is just another way to say that any human experience of God is bound to be an experience that transcends the human capacity for understanding.

This is also another way to remind ourselves that for all there is to be gained from the Scriptures, as well as from official church documents—such as the *Catechism of the Catholic Church* and the Vatican II documents—there comes a point in an adult spirituality where we set all human words and concepts aside. There comes a point where we use the Scriptures like a trampoline, to bounce up, up, and rest in darkness and unknowing, mid-air in the purity of God's presence beyond the limitations of all words and concepts.

The knowledge that comes from faith is a knowledge of the heart more than of the mind. It is the knowledge that, as St. Teresa of Avila said, "God is full of compassion," if only you "trust in him alone." This may sound like a comfort, but it is also a challenge. Think of how difficult it can be to trust in God *alone*. We are so inclined to trust in just about anything else as long as we can lay our hands on it, which we cannot do with God. Recall the old story about the hiker who slips over the edge of a steep canyon but manages to get a hold on a little tree. There the hiker dangles with a drop of hundreds of feet below. "Help!" the hiker cries, over and over. "Someone, please help me!" Then a voice says, "Let go, I'll catch you." The hiker replies, "Who are you?" The voice responds, "God. Let go, you'll be safe." After a pause, the hiker calls out, "Help! Is there anybody else there?"

The knowledge that faith gives is not a certainty we can grab and hold in our hands. Regardless of how much we say we trust in God, our trust is based on a form of knowledge—knowledge of God—for which we get little if any support from the dominant culture. Therefore, to live that trust is to oppose the dominant culture, an act guaranteed to make anyone feel anxious, fearful, and uncertain. That's the kind of power culture has in any human life. To oppose your culture is to oppose the meaning system that functions in virtually every aspect of your life. To place ultimate trust in God instead of in what the dominant culture places ultimate trust in—which in our case is financial forms of security—is to ask to be anxious, afraid, and uncertain most of the time, so great is the power of culture. It's unavoidable, and how long can anyone continue that way?

All the same, the knowledge that faith gives is a knowledge that constantly whispers in your ear to give ultimate trust in God a try. How about today? How about in this situation? You haven't tried it lately, so how about now? Trust in God, trust in God's love for you, trust in God alone. Try this instead of trusting only in money and other financial forms of security. It gives you the willies, but give it a try anyway. Maybe you'll be glad you did. Maybe it is true that "the love of money is a root of all kinds of evil . . ." (1 Timothy 6:10). What if St. Paul was right? What if his words are true, not just pious old words with no connection to the real world? What if?

Saints are people who took that little step away from the dominant culture of their time—call it "the world"—through the narrow door called Take a Chance, and into the wide open spaces of the knowledge of God and of the Really Real that faith gives to anyone who asks for it. Saints are ordinary people who believed more in the knowledge that faith gives than they believed in the dominant culture of their time and place. Saints are ordinary people for whom the knowledge that faith gives was Really Real, not just an ideal or a dream or wishful thinking. For them it was Real, so they did all kinds of simple things that in all times and places seem Unrealistic In The Extreme.

The Church is more than a human institution. But the Church is also, definitely, a human institution. Saints are ordinary people who believed that the Church as a human institution should try to take the gospel as if it is true; should trust more in God than in money, for example. God wants us to do this, they would say. But we don't have the money, the opponents would say. Do it and God will give the money, the saint would say, truly and really trusting that the knowledge that faith gives is Real. Act on the knowledge that faith gives, and invariably God will do his part. But no matter how often we hear such true stories we still believe that the knowledge that faith gives is wishful thinking, an unattainable ideal, a dream—a wonderful dream, a beautiful ideal, but unattainable all the same. Wishful thinking.

Saints are ordinary people whose faith knowledge made the gospel so real for them that they had no trouble speaking such messages even to bishops and popes. Of course, this got them into trouble, as it gets saints in all times and places into trouble. Far from being a kind of esoteric secret knowledge, the knowledge that faith gives is practically guaranteed to get you into trouble if you act on it as the foundation for your life.

Can the knowledge that comes from authentic faith be put into clearly understandable words, sentences, and paragraphs? Can this knowledge be so stated that its rationale will be convincing to even the most hard-bitten skeptic? Sorry, but no. Words and phrases can only hint at the knowledge that faith gives, and the words and phrases that do this are loaded with analogies and metaphors—are, in fact, a simple kind of poetry that either touches your heart or does not touch your heart. This is so because the Christian religion is not primarily an intellectual system. It's poetry.[2]

The knowledge that faith gives comes not from outside of and with no connection to the created order—as with Gnosticism. Rather, the knowledge that comes from faith comes through a system of symbols and signs. But these are not "merely" symbols and signs. Rather, these symbols and signs are special because they open up and reveal the holy, the sacred in the world, in the universe, in all things human, and in all things in space and time. Catholicism, in particular, is a vast and variegated poem that evokes, "What no eye has seen, nor ear heard, nor the human heart conceived, what God has prepared for those who love him" (1 Corinthians 2:9).

The knowledge that faith brings is, for the Christian, knowledge of the gospel as the key to eternal life in this world and the next. Remember that *eternal* is not a mere synonym for *forever*. Rather, *eternal* means "having neither beginning nor end but being unchangeably full of life."³ Eternity only truly exists in God, but in Christ God allows us to share in eternal life. "I am the resurrection and the life," Jesus tells the Samaritan woman in the Gospel of John. "Those who believe in me, even though they die, will live, and everyone who lives and believes in me will never die" (11:25–26).

Faith gives the knowledge that, contrary to appearances, to live in Christ is to share in eternal life, that is, God's own life that has no beginning and no end. The knowledge that faith gives is the knowledge that this is not just a dreamy idea but an accomplished fact. Consequently, the believer finds it possible to live—or at least strive to live—as if this is not a dream but reality.

The mistaken notion that faith brings, or should bring, some form of secret, esoteric knowledge concerning What It's All About does authentic faith no great service. Fundamentally, the knowledge that faith gives is not cognitive or intellectual except in a derivative or secondary sense. The knowledge that faith gives is more an awareness of God's presence and activity in your life, in human lives in general, and in the world. Knowledge and acceptance of particular doctrines, teachings, or beliefs depends entirely upon this awareness as an ongoing basis for your life.

In a nutshell, the knowledge that Christian faith gives is knowledge of God and of the Risen Christ, and it's a knowledge available to anyone. As we read in the Gospel of John: "And this is eternal life, that they may know you, the only true God, and Jesus Christ whom you have sent" (17:3).

3

Faith is not
an ideology

A dictionary defines *ideology* thus: "A set of doctrines or beliefs that form the basis of a political, economic, or other system."[1] An ideology is a set of ideas or perspectives according to which those who accept that ideology evaluate and either accept or reject all other ideas and perspectives. For someone who is an ideologue there is no room for a variety of acceptable points of view or a pluralistic outlook on life and the world. Instead, if an idea or perspective is incompatible with his or her ideology, that makes it not just different but wrong or false.

Faith becomes an ideology when and if you equate your faith with a particular theological perspective according to which there is no room for other theological perspectives or interpretations; all theological points of view are invalid except your own. The temptation to allow faith to become an ideology is both subtle and insidious, not just among various religious traditions but within particular religious traditions, as well.

In our era, for example, ideological interpretations of, or perspectives on, Catholicism are common—and not just among theologians. Ideological interpretations of Catholicism in parishes are not uncommon. Thus, in population centers of any size at all you are bound to find parishes that are known to be "liberal" or "conservative." In both cases, you will find that the life of the parish is guided by a particular theological ideology, or by a particular ideological interpretation of faith and of what it means to be Catholic.

A parish where a liberal Catholic theological ideology dominates will, most likely, give considerable attention to social justice issues. Such a parish will also demonstrate considerable open-mindedness about ecumenical exchanges with other churches and other religions. The liturgies at a liberal parish will most likely "push the envelope" when it comes to incorporating changes that do not have official church approval. These changes may include the use of liturgical prayers culled from sources other than the Sacramentary, the incorporation of feminine images for God into liturgical prayers, and the modification of traditional ritual prayer formulas—such as the baptismal ritual—to reflect the parish's dominant liberal theological ideology. Also, there will be either no altar servers at all, or more girls than boys will participate in this liturgical role. Liturgical music is invariably "progressive," and on any given Sunday you are more likely to hear guitars and flutes than an organ. In radically liberal settings, groups may reject all traditional structures and, for example, designate a woman, a laicized priest, or a nonordained man to preside at a "eucharist."

In a parish where a conservative Catholic theological ideology holds sway, you will probably hear a good deal about opposition to abortion, contraception, and homosexual activity. Official church documents, such as the *Catechism of the Catholic Church*, are likely to be a focus of attention. Liturgically, a conservative theological ideology will dictate strict adherence to official church guidelines, unless those guidelines drift in a liberal direction. A conservative parish will, most likely, not allow girls to be altar servers, even though official church directives allow this. Conservative parishes may still have an altar rail between the sanctuary and the main body of the church, and people may kneel at the altar rail to receive Communion. Depending on how conservative the parish is, women may not serve as lectors or eucharistic ministers to help distribute Communion. Liturgical music in a conservative parish will probably be limited to traditional hymns accompanied by an organ.

Behind both ultra-liberal and ultra-conservative Catholic theological ideologies you will find certain images of the church, or ecclesiologies (theologies of the Church). To borrow images made popular by Cardinal Avery Dulles, S.J., in his book *Models of the Church*, an ultra-liberal view of the Church will emphasize the Church as "community of disciples and servant," and "building community" will be a dominant theme.[2] Interaction with other people will be encouraged in liturgical and social situations. In so far as possible, the local parish community will be the exclusive focus, and few opportunities will be missed to downplay identification with the Vatican, the pope, or the worldwide Catholic Church. Some ultra-liberal parishes will have little, if any, shared devotional life, and the cultivation of a devotional component of a personal spirituality may receive little, if any, attention. Ideally, because of the emphasis on social justice and a spirit of community that embraces the marginalized, liberal parishes will have a lively shared devotional life, but this is not always so. Instead, the emphasis may tend to be on shared social action rather than shared devotional prayer times.

An ultra-conservative parish will emphasize the Church as "institution and mystical communion." Obedience to official church teachings will be emphasized, and there will be frequent opportunities to participate in communal devotional activities. The dominant assumption regarding liturgy may be that the primary purpose of liturgical activities is communion with God, and while this communion occurs in communal gatherings, an ultra-conservative Catholic might tend to view it as inappropriate for liturgies to include an emphasis on human interaction during the liturgy itself.

An ideology is difficult to argue with because it is based upon certain presuppositions that can be neither proved nor disproved. You either accept or reject these presuppositions, and typically your reasons for doing so are more emotional and psychological than intellectual. An ideology is rarely, if ever, the result of a rational process that leads to this particular ideology. Rather, any rational argument mustered to defend an ideology comes after the fact, to defend the ideology and, sometimes, to attack those who don't agree with you.

For those whose faith is an ultra-conservative Catholic ideology, their ideology is based on unprovable presuppositions such as, "The pope's teachings are to be followed to the letter because when the pope speaks that's as close as we can get in this life to hearing God speak."

For a faith that is an ultra-liberal Catholic ideology, underlying unprovable presuppositions include: "The pope's teachings are merely his human opinion, so we need to think things through for ourselves and do what we conclude is right."

Another way in which faith can become an ideology is when a person's faith is focused exclusively, or almost exclusively, on one issue so that issue becomes the measuring stick against which everything else is evaluated. The issue may be a "conservative" issue—such as the Church's official teaching against the use of artificial contraceptives, or against abortion. Or, the issue may be a "liberal" issue—such as the Church's official teaching which virtually rules out capital punishment, support for a ministry to homosexuals that does not try to get them to abandon homosexual genital activity, or the incorporation of gender inclusive language, with regard to God, into the Bible and all liturgical texts.

Whatever the issue, if faith becomes too focused on that issue, the result is an ideological faith. Such a person implicitly condemns anyone who disagrees with his or her position on this particular issue. Thus, for some people, you are a bad Catholic if you "support a woman's right to choose [i.e., abortion]." For others, you are a bad Catholic if you oppose the introduction of gender-inclusive language with regard to God into the Bible and the liturgy. In fact, any faith that is too focused on a single issue is less than Catholic.

A Catholic faith cannot be an ideological faith. *Catholic* means "universal" and "all-encompassing." Sometimes you hear the phrase "narrow-minded Catholic," but this is an oxymoron of gargantuan proportions. No faith that is genuinely Catholic can be narrow-minded; no faith that is genuinely Catholic can be ideological. A Catholic faith is, by its very nature, a faith open to goodness, truth, and beauty no matter what the immediate source, because the ultimate source of all goodness, truth, and beauty is God.

Not only that, but a Catholic faith cannot be genuinely Catholic and be intolerant of opinions and points of view that differ from your own. G. K. Chesterton, the great early twentieth-century English convert to Catholicism, once said: "Catholics know the two or three transcendental truths upon which they do agree; and take rather a pleasure in disagreeing on everything else."[3] In other words, a Catholic faith that is genuine finds it perfectly possible to disagree without hurling anathemas in all directions. In the best of all possible churches, conservatives and liberals should be able to disagree and still maintain good humor.

Back in the waning years of the twentieth century, it came to me that I might be able to encourage some of this good humor. Tongue firmly planted in cheek, I sent out a media release to Catholic newspapers and magazines announcing that I had established the Grim Catholic Institute. Annually, I would announce the winner of the Grim Catholic Award, to be given to a prominent Catholic who, by his or her words and actions, best exemplified during the previous year the direct opposite of the joy evident in the example and teachings of the Jesus of the Gospels. The winner of the award could be either a liberal or conservative Catholic, since both camps tend to produce more than their share of grim Catholics.

It soon became evident, however, that the Grim Catholic Award had no future. I had to cancel the award "on account of grimness." Neither conservative nor liberal journalists thought my idea was humorous. The editors of both liberal and conservative newspapers greeted the announcement of the award with grimness. One editor, after I tried to explain what I was doing, said, "What's the point? I don't get it."

Catholic grimness was far more rampant than I had thought. Catholic journalists, at least of the extreme liberal and conservative varieties, have little sense of humor unless you poke fun at the opposite extreme. A liberal Catholic can laugh at jokes about conservative Catholics, and a conservative Catholic can laugh at jokes about liberal Catholics, but there I was asking both to laugh at themselves—and that was asking too much, because it would mean abandoning their respective ideological positions. Once faith becomes an ideology it has no sense of humor at all.

In truth, genuine faith is ever ready to laugh at itself because it knows that the human concepts it formulates about itself are but feeble attempts to think and talk about a Reality and an experience no human concepts can ever pin down. Genuine faith has a great sense of humor, can laugh at itself, because it brings you into communion with God, the Divine Mystery, who/which can never be captured by even the most orthodox of orthodoxies, even the most carefully thought-out doctrines or the most brilliant theological system. Genuine faith can laugh at itself because, in the famous words of St. Thomas Aquinas (1225–1275) concerning all the works of his theological genius: "All that I have written appears to me as much straw after the things that have been revealed to me."[4]

Faith, if it is genuine, never confuses itself with human concepts used to talk about faith. Therefore, it cannot become an ideology. Therefore, it retains its sense of humor. Faith is one thing; the words we use to talk about faith are another thing. This is what Aquinas saw so clearly at the end of his life. As long as you can distinguish between your faith and human words and thoughts *about* faith, your faith will never become an ideology.

Of course, you may say, Thomas Aquinas was a saint, and he said that divine mysteries were revealed to him, so it was easy for him to say that in comparison all his theological writings looked like straw. But we are not saints, and we haven't had any divine revelations lately. So it's difficult for us to not get attached to human concepts when it comes to our faith. It's difficult for us to not get defensive when someone seems to attack our understanding of faith, and the Church, and so forth, and if that means our faith has become an ideology, well, there is not much we can do about that. We are not going to let someone verbally stomp all over what we understand real faith to be.

Point well taken. All the same, it's not entirely true that God does not reveal divine things to us ordinary folks. In fact, anyone with a spiritual life that is even half alive and kicking has divine revelations on a daily basis; they just don't realize it. All it takes to short-circuit an ideological faith is to become aware that you are a mystic. A mystic, you? Yes, you. Mysticism is far more common than we think it is.

Have you ever felt loved by another person? That was God's love you felt, too. Do you ever take a deep breath, exhale, and feel better for having done that? That was God's presence that you inhaled, that entered and refreshed you. Is there some activity in your life that, most of the time, you would rather engage in than anything else? Do you have an invisible version of one of those bumper stickers that declare, "I'd rather be [insert favorite activity here]"? Perhaps you'd rather be quilting, gardening, sailing, walking, or reading. The reason you have a passion for any activity or interest is that you find God in that activity or interest. That's how we are put together.

I myself had an experience that may be instructive here, and I draw on the familiar opening words of Dante's *Divine Comedy* to illustrate what I mean:

Midway upon the journey of our life
I found myself within a forest dark,
For the straightforward pathway had been lost.[5]

Midway upon the journey of my life, one day suddenly—and I do mean suddenly, but it was like a nagging voice prodding me to act before it was too late—I knew it was time. For nearly thirty years, I had been attracted by the idea of learning to play the five-string banjo. What with marriage, three sons, and a busy work schedule, however, I never did anything about this attraction. Then one day, at the age of fifty-three, I knew the time was right. Our three sons were young adults, so I had some time I could use to act on my decades-long fantasy and learn to play the five-string banjo. Slumbering in my soul for lo, those many years, my wish to play the banjo came alive like a phoenix ready to take flight, and when it did it became not just a casual interest but a passion.

The "straightforward path" I had been on for years and years took a 180-degree detour, and the five-string banjo became my preoccupation. From that time on, every spare moment became time I could use to practice the banjo, and the reason was that in my passion for the banjo I connected with the joyful, celebrating, life-is-worth-living Divine Mystery that we call God. You might say that in my passion for the five-string banjo I found a sacrament (lower case "s"), a way to be more alive, more in touch with life itself. When I practice the basic "rolls"—rhythmic patterns for "picking" or plucking the strings of the banjo—and when I practice, and practice, and practice a tune I want to be able to play, something bigger happens. I feel a joy in living that I don't find in other activities. Unfortunately, the same may not be true for others who can't help but listen to my less than dulcet tones!

All the same, playing the five-string banjo, for me, is a kind of mysticism, and your passion, no matter how "secular" and ordinary it may seem, whether it's quilting or cooking, gardening or painting pictures, is your mysticism, too—your way of feeling closer to God and more alive than at other times in your life. This is the "revelation," if you will, that makes it possible—just as Aquinas's revelations made it possible for him—to recognize that all conceptualizations of faith are "straw." Your way of being a mystic, your way of feeling "up close and personal" with God, is what makes it possible for you to resist the inclination to let your faith become an ideology. You know, because of what has been revealed to you, that if you let your faith become an ideology, you worship not God but words about God.

We can't do without our words about God, of course. Indeed, our metaphors and analogies are indispensable when it comes to being in relation to God. Metaphors and analogies mediate God to us in ways nothing else can do. Our *experiences* of God—in my case, my passion for playing the five-string banjo—help make it possible to recognize that metaphors and analogies have their limits, that they are not ends in themselves, or absolutes. Metaphors and analogies mediate God to us, they are not God.

Of course, it's not as if a passionate enjoyment of quilting, gardening, tinkering with old cars, or playing the five-string banjo is the only way we have to be mystics and experience God. Being with a friend or watching the stars in a night sky can do the same. A loving marriage can be an ongoing experience of God's presence, and the experience of sexual love in marriage can lead to peak moments, mysticism-wise. The point is that everyone knows moments of great joy when God feels close, and these moments help keep any verbalization about God in its proper balance. Such moments help us—or *should* help us—keep our words about faith from becoming an ideology.

Of course, this does not always prove to be the case. For some people, the emotional or psychological need for absolute certainty is so great that they can't help but cling to an ideological faith. If this ideological faith is Catholic, it will be either quite liberal or quite conservative, because an ideology is by its very nature extreme and uncompromising. The emotional need for security is so great that it uses the certainty of a conservative or liberal faith to protect itself from uncertainty in an uncertain world.

Only an ideological faith can provide certainty, which is why it appeals to those with a psychological need for certainty. Authentic faith, on the contrary, is anything but a source of certainty. A story about the great twentieth-century novelist and Catholic convert Graham Greene will illustrate the point:

> Greene often discussed his problems of faith and belief with Father Leopoldo Duran, a close friend during the last quarter-century of his life. Duran recalled a particularly poignant moment after breakfast on July 8, 1987: "Each day I have less and less faith," said Greene. Duran replied,

"Yes, but you have often told me that with every passing
day you find you have less 'belief,' but more 'faith.'" Greene
was silent, then uttered what Duran said was the most perfect remark on the subject: "The trouble is, I don't believe
my unbelief." (According to Duran, when faith seemed to
have disappeared, Greene told God: "Lord, I offer you my
unbelief.")[6]

Although it isn't clear exactly how Graham Greene understood the
distinction between faith and belief, it may have been a distinction
between belief in the institutional elements of Catholic religious life
and faith in God directly. At any rate, the trouble is that authentic faith
is never easy to pin down or put in a bottle or measure with a yardstick.
But an ideological faith is easy to pin down, which is what makes it
attractive. You can trot out an ideological faith like a pet that you keep
in a cage. An ideological faith offers no surprises, only predictability.
An ideological faith is like a suit of armor you wear to protect yourself
from just about everything, whereas authentic faith is like going out
into the world each day unprotected. An ideological faith is a spiritual
insurance policy, while authentic faith turns you into a risk taker.

With Graham Greene, authentic faith does not believe its own
unbelief—and authentic faith experiences plenty of unbelief. That's
one of the big differences between an ideological faith and authentic
faith: authentic faith includes and is not surprised by—nor does it
worry about—unbelief. Belief is mental, while faith is personal. Belief
is a "head trip," while authentic faith is a "heart trip." Faith becomes
ideological if you confuse faith with belief, because belief grasps for
certainty while faith loses itself in trust and self-abandonment to God.

Is there no sense in which faith brings certainty? None at all? Faith
does bring a sort of certainty, but it is not the kind of certainty that
comes from being absolutely sure about anything. Rather, the certainty that you get from authentic faith is the certainty that, ultimately,
God will not betray your trust; that, in the end, everything will be
okay. For authentic faith, however, along the way there is no certainty at all. All hell can, and may, break loose along the way, between here
and there. But that is the difference between authentic faith and ideological faith. The former continues to trust even when all hell breaks
loose; the latter gives up in despair. Authentic faith kids around with
the executioner and meets death as a friend. Ideological faith spits in

the executioner's eye and dies a bitter death. Authentic faith is St. Thomas More joking with the headsman to do no harm to his long beard, since it had done no wrong. Of course, there is also a perfectly serious sense in which authentic faith is willing to die for Christ— which is exactly what Thomas More did.

An ideological faith puts its hope and trust in certain principles, a set of specific theological, social, political, and economic principles. Authentic faith puts it hope and trust in God alone. Oh, authentic faith has theological, social, political, and economic principles, to be sure. But authentic faith does not see its principles as infallible or absolute. Ideological faith cherishes its principles as absolute and infallible, and when its principles fail or the rest of the world does not embrace its principles, it grows angry. Ideological faith requires the approval of no one, and ideological faith rejects the role of any authority because it is so certain of its own self-righteousness.

Ideological faith is stiff-necked and arrogant. Authentic faith is familiar with humility, and even when it has the truth it is willing to step down, or step aside, or give way when legitimate authority dictates that it must do so—even when "legitimate authority" is wrong and does not have the truth. Authentic faith refuses to think and act as if the truth depends upon its own words and actions. Authentic faith knows that the truth will come out, will surface, will rise to the top, sooner or later, and that this does not depend upon it becoming arrogant.

Authentic faith is the Jesuit Pierre Teilhard de Chardin bowing to the wishes of legitimate church authorities, in the 1950s, to not publish his amazing, groundbreaking work. His blend of science and theology was so new and original that no one knew what to think of it. He knew that his writings would be published eventually if they were good and true, and that was all that mattered to him. So his books, including *The Phenomenon of Man*, *The Divine Milieu*, and *Hymn of the Universe*, were published, alright, but after his death.

Authentic faith is the Trappist monk, Thomas Merton, bowing to the wishes of his Trappist superiors that he not publish certain of his writings on peace and nuclear warfare during the 1950s and '60s. They thought Merton was outside the monastic tradition and outside the Church's theology when, in fact, he was closer to the heart of the tradition and the Church's theology than anyone else at the time. Merton knew his superiors were small-minded, but he also did not have an ideological faith, so he could leave it all to God. In the end, his writings on peace were published because the good and the true cannot be hidden forever, for example, *Merton on Peace.*

The long and the short of it is that an ideological faith is the faith of a person who worships his or her own ideas, principles, and opinions, while authentic faith worships a God who is Love. Authentic faith cannot be ideological because authentic faith will settle for God alone. Authentic faith cannot be ideological because it knows that anything short of God—including ideas, principles, and opinions—too easily becomes a false god, and authentic faith will have nothing to do with the worship of false gods. Authentic faith knows that the long and the short of it is that only God can be trusted, and when push comes to shove God has no need for you to get pushy with your ideas, principles, and opinions.

Perhaps the ultimate test of whether or not a faith is ideological is this: if you are willing to declare seriously, from the heart, that you could be wrong, and if you are willing to change when and where you see that you are wrong, then your faith—whether of a liberal or a conservative bent—is not ideological.

Faith is not
a security blanket

The term *security blanket* originated in the late Charles Schulz's popular comic strip, *Peanuts*. Schulz's cartoon characters never actually used the term *security blanket*, but the metaphor itself came from there. All of Schulz's characters were precocious children, of course. But Linus retained the particularly childish habit of clinging to his blanket and sucking his thumb, all the while speaking in a precocious manner.

In some of the strips, Schulz's dog character, Snoopy, tried to snatch Linus's blanket from him and run away with it. Snoopy would streak by Linus, grab the blanket in his teeth, and keep on going. Often, however, Linus would hang onto the blanket and become airborne as Snoopy dashed away with the other end of the blanket in his jaws. At other times, Linus would notice that Snoopy was about to try to get his blanket away from him, and would warn the dog that dire consequences would result if he followed through on his plan.

The remarkable thing about this whole situation in the *Peanuts* comic strip was the tenacity with which Linus—a consistently intelligent and common-sense character in the strip—clung to his blanket, no matter what. Even Snoopy could see that it was not healthy for Linus to depend on his blanket so much. All the same, Linus would not part with his blanket once he had it in his hands. Of course, there were many *Peanuts* strips featuring Linus in which the blanket did not appear. Often, it seems, Linus left his blanket at home. At the same time, Schulz often portrayed Linus as the most religious of his characters. Linus, for example, was the one who could quote Scripture for just about any situation.[1] In the famous made-for-television *Peanuts* movie, *A Charlie Brown Christmas*, it's Linus who stands on stage and recites the narrative about the birth of Jesus from the Gospel of Luke.

That Linus was both the most articulate *Peanuts* character when it came to religion, and the character who turned to his blanket most often for security, may not have been a mere coincidence. Maybe Charles Schulz perceived a fairly common connection between religion and a need for a false sense of security. Perhaps he saw that people quite often use their faith much as Linus used his blanket, as a source of security. Yet, as anyone can see, this is a childish thing to do because a blanket is no source of real security. A blanket gives nothing but a sensate feeling, and a sensate feeling isn't real security at all.

Perhaps by pairing religion and a reliance on a security blanket in one character, Charles Schulz wanted to get religious people to ask questions about allowing faith to become a kind of security blanket. Perhaps he wanted to help us see that a faith that is a security blanket is no real faith at all, but an illusion. Of course, there is a way in which we can say that faith is a source of security, but we must quickly add that faith is a source of *ultimate* security, and that makes a significant difference.

When we say that faith is not a security blanket, the metaphor of the security blanket is an image of a faith that you can turn to anytime for a feeling of well-being. All you need to do is grab your faith and pop a thumb in your mouth to make things right with the world. But if this is how you relate to your faith, then your faith is bound to disappoint you. If, when life gets scary, you turn to your faith, like Linus turns to his blanket, sooner or later you will discover that your faith will slip right through your fingers and be gone. Sooner or later, life, like Snoopy, will snatch your security-blanket faith away from you, and because it is a weak kind of faith, it will be gone in the blink of an eye. Zip! Gone, just like Snoopy is gone with Linus's blanket. Of course, you may try to hang on to your security-blanket faith, but if you do, you can expect to find yourself airborne and going for a wild ride; before long your security-blanket faith will slip from your grasp and be gone, with you lying on the ground wondering what the heck happened.

A security-blanket faith is phony because it is a "faith" that depends upon a woefully inadequate image of God. It reduces God to the role of an emergency rescue technician. If my faith is a security blanket, then it is God's role to rescue me from bad times, suffering, grief, and the consequences of my own stupid mistakes and idiotic choices. Hanging on to a security-blanket faith means that my faith will never require me to take any risks or accept suffering for the sake of some greater good. A security-blanket faith implies that Jesus doesn't mean it when, in the Gospels, he says such things as:

> "Blessed are those who are persecuted for righteousness' sake, for theirs is the kingdom of heaven.
> "Blessed are you when people revile you and persecute you and utter all kinds of evil against you falsely on my account" (Matthew 5:10–11).

Perhaps even more to the point, Jesus' words about a faith that is inadequate could easily describe a security-blanket faith:

> "But they have no root, and endure only for a while; then, when trouble or persecution arises on account of the word, immediately they fall away" (Mark 4:17).

Authentic Christian faith simply is not a security-blanket faith because such a faith is unreliable and does not last. Anyone who lives an authentic faith—as Jesus' words above from the Gospel of Mark illustrate—is bound to encounter not less but more trouble, so how could such a faith be a security blanket?

One of the best-known statements about faith in Scripture comes from the so-called letter to the Hebrews, and it goes like this: "Now faith is the assurance of things hoped for, the conviction of things not seen" (11:1).[2]

A security-blanket faith, on the contrary, is the assurance of things you have in your grasp, the conviction of things you can see plainly. In other words, a security-blanket faith is an illusory faith.

Once there was a woman of considerable means. In fact, she was—to borrow words from a song in the 1960s musical play, "Stop the World, I Want to Get Off"—"dirty rotten filthy stinking rich." This woman had money to burn, and she regularly burned it with gusto. She wallowed in the lap of luxury. You name it, goodies-wise, and she had it. All the best, all the latest, all the most beautiful, all the most fun. At the same time, Ms. Money Bags was also full of darkness and gloom. She smiled on the outside, cried on the inside. In her heart it was sadness and despair most of the time.

What made this even more complicated was that Ms. Money Bags was a religious person. A Catholic religious person, even. She attended Mass, not just on Sundays but every day of the week. Your basic daily communicant. And why did she go to Mass every day? I'll tell you. She went to Mass every day because she wanted God to take care of a few things for her in a few departments where her money had no power to change anything. Like, her husband was so insensitive. Like, her two grown sons were a Big Disappointment to her, and likewise her grown daughter. Big Disappointments, all three of them.

So the woman went to Mass every day, and when she received Communion, she prayed to the Lord Jesus that he would make her husband more sensitive toward her, maybe bring her a rose now and then. She prayed that one son would stop living in sin with his girl-friend. She prayed that the other son would stop smoking and go back to college. She prayed that her daughter would stop smoking and get a job and stop living at home, sponging off her parents. She prayed that God would not let her children remain away from the Catholic religion, that he would bring them back to the Church and not let them wander through life without the light of the Catholic faith to guide them. Every day when she received Communion, Ms. Money Bags prayed earnestly for these things to happen. She prayed the same prayers over and over to the Lord Jesus.

For two years the woman went to Mass every day and prayed for the same things, for her husband, for her sons and her daughter—but what she prayed for never happened. Then one day, the woman realized that her prayers were not being answered. She was not getting what she asked for. Her husband did not bring her a rose. Her sons and her daughter went on with their lives as before, and nothing changed. With this realization, Ms. Money Bags grew more and more gloomy about it all, and then one day she decided to stop going to Mass on weekdays. Nuts. If God wasn't going to do what she asked, and make her husband and her sons and daughters do what she want-ed, then she was not about to keep going to Mass and praying. If her prayers were not answered after two years, why should she keep it up?

It was like banging her head against a wall. But first, Ms. Money Bags thought she would talk with someone else about it.

Ms. Money Bags knew a woman named Carol from her parish because Carol occasionally called Ms. Money Bags to ask for donations for various charitable causes—requests Ms. Money Bags responded to with donations half as large as they should have been. Ms. Money Bags recalled that Carol seemed to have a kind of "spiritual" quality about her, so maybe she would tell her why her prayers had not been answered.

Ms. Money Bags called Carol, who suggested they get together for lunch later that week. They met at a soup-and-sandwich shop, and once they had their sandwiches and beverages, Ms. Money Bags neglected hers and talked while Carol ate. She explained how she'd been praying for two years with no results. Why did God ignore her prayers when the things she prayed for were obviously good? After finishing a bite of her sandwich and sipping from her glass of lemonade, Carol shrugged her shoulders and offered, "I haven't the foggiest idea."

Ms. Money Bags was aghast. Carol went on: "Personally, I believe that God wants to hear from us about our specific concerns and worries, but he also wants us to say thank you, now and then, for the good things we do have. As far as your prayers are concerned, maybe you're being too specific, or at least maybe your prayers are incomplete. It's fine to tell God what you think he should do with regard to your husband and kids, but I try to always end my prayers for specifics with a more general prayer, something like, 'Loving God, please give these people the kinds of healing and liberation you know each one needs the most. Save each one in the ways you know he or she needs most to be saved, and I leave it all in your hands. Amen.' That kind of thing. That way, you leave the specifics to God, and your main issue becomes trusting in God, which, ultimately, is the main issue anyway. At least, that's what I think. Aren't you going to eat your sandwich?"

"But . . ." said Ms. Money Bags vacantly.

"You know what I think?" Carol asked. "I think that if the main purpose of our prayers is to tell God exactly what to do, then we don't really want to let God be God. It means that, in effect, we want to be God, which means that our faith is nothing but a spiritual security blanket, something to protect us from bad times and bleak tomorrows, and a faith like this isn't really faith at all because it requires no trust."

Ms. Money Bags was devastated. She did not eat her sandwich, so Carol wrapped it up and took it home for later. Ms. Money Bags drove home in a daze.

When faith is a security blanket, it becomes something you try to wrap yourself in, something to bundle up in to keep warm and cozy, something to rely upon when all your other resources are exhausted or don't do any good. Ms. Money Bags used her faith this way, as a source of control or power when her money failed her or could do no more. Finally, when her faith didn't function the way she wanted it to—by taking care of the problems her money could do nothing about—she began to give up on her faith.

The ever-popular St. Thérèse of Lisieux (1873–1897) was a simple young woman who took simple, everyday situations and turned them into profoundly important ones. She wrote:

> O how glorious our Faith is! Instead of restricting hearts, as the world fancies, it uplifts them and enlarges their capacity to love, to love with an almost infinite love, since it will continue unbroken beyond our mortal life.[3]

A security-blanket faith restricts you, for that is the nature of a blanket—to cover you and keep you from moving much, for it must do this to keep you warm and protected. In fact, this is one way you can tell if your faith has become a security blanket. If you rarely find that your faith sparks free movement, rarely find yourself engaged in activities on behalf of others that are out of the ordinary, rarely do anything that is not implicitly approved by the dominant popular culture, chances are your faith has become a security blanket. In fact, taken to an extreme, a security blanket becomes . . . a straitjacket.

A straitjacket, of course, is a long-sleeved jacket-like garment used to bind the arms tightly against the body. Somebody had the bright idea to design such a garment to restrain a violent patient or prisoner. But the point is, a straitjacket restricts, hinders, or confines, and a faith that is a security blanket can easily become a faith that is a straitjacket, a faith that restricts, that hinders or confines, that may tie you up in knots. Instead of liberating and healing, a straitjacket faith makes it practically impossible to move with freedom. A person wearing a straitjacket is safe and secure, but he or she is also incapable of acting freely.

Clung to long enough, a security-blanket faith is guaranteed to become a straitjacket faith, and a straitjacket faith is hardly a source of freedom and joy. Consider these words of St. Paul: "For freedom Christ has set us free. Stand firm, therefore, and do not submit again to a yoke of slavery" (Galatians 5:1a).

The "slavery" Paul refers to is, of course, a legalistic faith, a faith that depends on laws, rules, and regulations to know what and what not to do. Just a few verses later, Paul says, "You who want to be justified by the law have cut yourselves off from Christ; you have fallen away from grace" (Galatians 5:4). For St. Paul, the "yoke of slavery" is another metaphor for what we are calling a security-blanket faith and a straitjacket faith. Someone who is a slave, or wearing a straitjacket, is secure, oh yes. There is a real kind of security that comes with being a slave or wearing a straitjacket. In the former case, your master will see to that. In the latter, your caretakers put you in a straitjacket so you cannot harm yourself, so they make certain that no other kind of harm comes to you.

A legalistic faith offers the same kind of security, the kind of security that comes from slavery or a straitjacket. As St. Paul understood, a legalistic faith enslaves you to legalism. You can't make a move unless the rules and regulations allow for it—and when they do allow movement, you can be confident and feel safe knowing that you understand exactly what God wants you to do and not do. Thus, you are not only safe and secure here and now but safe and secure for all eternity. Your legalistic faith gives you complete certainty, total confidence, and freedom from all doubt. You know what God wants and does not want because the rules and regulations tell you so. You are safe and secure, but your safety and security are those of a slave, those of someone confined to a straitjacket.

To return to our original metaphor, however, we can now see that a security-blanket faith is an unreliable faith. A security-blanket faith is an illusion because it is a faith that confines rather than liberates. A security-blanket faith keeps you bundled up, it does not liberate you. A security-blanket faith gives you all the answers and leaves you with no doubts—which is precisely why a security-blanket faith is an illusion that leaves you worshiping not the true God but an *idea* of God, a God who only gives rules and regulations that protect you from doubt *because they protect you from God.*

When finite beings, such as ourselves, encounter an infinite being, such as God is, it is impossible for finite beings to completely grasp or understand the infinite being, for the finite cannot grasp the infinite. As far as we humans are concerned, this means that faith always includes doubt. Doubt is a constitutive part of authentic faith. No doubt, no authentic faith. A faith devoid of doubts and questions is no longer authentic faith but something else: a security blanket, an ideology, or a spiritual aspirin, for starters. However, we'll save the final chapter in this book to get into faith and doubt in greater depth.

One of the most reliable signs of authentic faith is a life that includes risky choices that only faith can make sense out of. What risky choices? Consider the old question: If being a Christian were against the law, would there be enough evidence that you lived a Christian life to convict you in a court of law? Risky choices based on faith include the kinds of risks you take to give public witness on social justice issues, for example. This includes people who break laws to attract attention to injustices or to gain support for good causes of various kinds. It includes people who spend time in prison because they took such actions. But in the long run, in the big historical picture, such folks are the exception—prophetic witnesses whose witness is important, to be sure, but exceptions all the same.

More common are risky choices based on faith that seem so common that we rarely take notice of them. Take the choice to marry. When you choose not just *to marry*, but to marry *this particular person*, you take a huge risk that only a religious faith can support. Think about it. When you marry, you make an unconditional commitment to an imperfect relationship in an unpredictable world. Those whose choice to marry is a choice based on faith, ultimately based on trust in God, take a risk that is barely evident on the wedding day. But it is a risk all the same, and a big one. It's the kind of risk that is a sign of authentic faith, a faith that is no security blanket.

In truth, any major life choice based on faith is a risky choice characterized by considerable uncertainty. There is no way to be absolutely certain that you are making the right choice. All you can do is consider all the possibilities, gather as much information as you can, consult whatever sources of wisdom may be available—and then choose. The choice to become a priest or a religious is just as risky as the choice to marry. You put your life on the line, and the consequences are likely to be mixed, even when you make a good choice.

Indeed, only authentic faith makes it possible to cope in a positive, meaningful way with the "mixed-ness" of the consequences of our choices. In traditional Christian terms, any life choice is bound to lead to both joy and sorrow, darkness and light—to both cross and resurrection. Only faith can make sense of the sorrow and darkness that result from a life choice. Only faith can recognize and embrace the dimension of our choice that is symbolized by the cross. To marry is a joy, to be sure, but to marry is also to embrace the cross of Christ. To have children results in deep joy, but it sometimes results in deep pain as well. To become a priest or a religious, or to choose to remain single for life, is to choose a path that leads to both joy and sorrow. Only the eyes of faith can see in both cross and resurrection a life worth living, a commitment worth being faithful to for a lifetime.

If faith were a security blanket, then some of the most heroic examples of Christian holiness through the centuries missed the boat completely. I speak, of course, of the countless martyrs who died because they were Christians. Two modern examples are St. Maximilian Kolbe, the Polish Franciscan priest who, during World War II, volunteered to take the place of another man condemned to die by starvation in the infamous Nazi death camp, Auschwitz; and St. Edith Stein, a Jewish convert to Catholicism and Carmelite nun, who died in similar circumstances. By dying for their faith, both Maximilian Kolbe and Edith Stein followed in the footsteps of countless earlier Christian martyrs for whom faith was anything but a security blanket. Rather, for them faith was a one-way ticket to terrible suffering and death. Of course, you may suggest that in the long run faith was, indeed, a security blanket for such martyrs because it assured them of eternal safety and security. But to say this is to miss the point, for it is only faith that can "see" beyond death, precisely faith alone that allowed the Christian martyrs to trust in God's love to the extent that they were willing to give up everything, even life itself, for what their faith promised.

If faith were a security blanket, it would be nothing but a pathetic delusion and a poor substitute for a good, solid set of insurance policies. Indeed, insurance policies would be preferable to a security blanket faith because at least an insurance policy delivers on-the-spot cash if something unpleasant happens to you. Faith, on the other hand, will never deliver anything but ultimate freedom, ultimate healing, and a security that makes insecurity in this life unimportant in the long run.

Faith is not an escape clause or loophole

An escape clause and a loophole are not the same thing, although they are similar. An escape clause is a provision in a contract that specifies the conditions under which the one signing the contract is relieved of liability for failure to meet the terms of the contract. In other words, an escape clause is actually part of the contract that allows you to get out of the contract, right there in black and white for all to see.

A loophole, on the other hand, is a way of escaping a difficulty, especially an omission or ambiguity in the wording of a contract or law, that provides a means of evading compliance. In popular thought, a loophole is a way to avoid being responsible for something or a way to avoid the consequences of one's promises and actions.

A lifelong agnostic, the great vaudeville and early twentieth-century movie and radio comedian W. C. Fields was in the hospital for what would prove to be his final illness. Groucho Marx visited Fields and found him lying in bed reading a Bible. "Why Bill," Groucho said, "what are you doing?" To which Fields replied, "Looking for loopholes."

Faith is neither an escape clause nor a loophole. In the first place, faith is not a legalism at all. You don't agree to "have faith" or "believe" in order to "be saved." The Creator of the universe does not say to us, "Here's the deal. You believe in me and obey my rules, and you get to go to heaven after you die. Do not believe in me and disobey my rules, and you get a hell of a time for eternity."

Faith is not one side of a contract with God that allows you to have a happier, more pleasant, more pain-free existence than people who do not agree to "have faith." Faith does not give you an advantage in the game of life; it's not like a handicap in golf. Faith does not put you in a better position vis-á-vis life's troubles and trials so that God will help you have fewer troubles and trials than unbelievers. Faith does not guarantee that you will have more fun and more money than those who do not "have faith."

Here is what is at the root of the inclination to think of faith as an escape clause or loophole: the wish to have your cake and eat it too. To illustrate, the great twentieth-century philosopher and novelist Albert Camus once quipped, "Everyone would like to behave like a pagan, with everyone else behaving like a Christian."

To think of faith as an escape clause is to think that by "believing" you can write into your life a clause that will allow you to get away with nearly any behavior you like and still be welcome at heaven's gates when you die. To think of faith as an escape clause is to act as if God is a cosmic trickster who forces a contract on you called "life," and the consequences are guaranteed to be grim, but life comes with an escape clause, see, called "faith," see, that allows you to wiggle out of life's grimness like a pass in a game of Monopoly that allows you to pass Go and collect $200.

In his remarkable novel *Mr. White's Confession*, Robert Clark tells the story of Herbert White, a not overly bright but good-hearted man who, by following his instincts for doing good and trusting others, is unjustly sent to prison for many years.[1] Convicted of murdering Ruby Fahey, a young woman for whom he felt a great deal of affection, a woman he would not have harmed for anything in the world, Herbert White is finally proven innocent, released from prison, and able to return to his home town. The final sentence in the novel reads:

> Herbert White himself was left alone with only the love of
> Ruby and without the clear memory of her; and that love

was indistinguishable from all the other love and beauty that might be, from what glimmered in the trees, from the light shaking down out of the coloring leaves.[2]

If faith were an escape clause, Herbert White would not be sentenced to many years in prison for following his natural inclination to act in a trusting manner, and if it were a loophole he would be released after only a few days or weeks. Instead, Herbert White lives out his years in prison quietly and, when finally released, he finds himself mysteriously, mystically united with what Dante, in his *Divine Comedy*, called "the Love that moves the sun and the other stars." Herbert White's love for the long-dead Ruby Fahey is "indistinguishable from all the other love and beauty that might be . . ." Yet his faith, which remains inarticulate and implicit throughout the novel, does not save him from suffering. Instead, by being precisely what it is, it brings him into union with love and beauty itself—in other words, with God.

It is of the very nature of faith that it is not an escape clause and is not a loophole. For if it were, it would not be faith. Another example from fiction is Clyde Edgerton's delightful novel, *Walking Across Egypt*.[3] Edgerton tells the story of Mattie Rigsbee, of Listre, North Carolina, who is an amazing cook and has a penchant for opening her home to stray dogs.

Mattie takes a shine to a teenage delinquent named Wesley Benfield, who arrives to take advantage of Mattie and ends up being won over by her love . . . and her cooking. In the end, Wesley makes some choices that put him behind bars, but Mattie won't give up on him, no matter what. Even at the end of the story, with Wesley back in jail and the stray dog back in the animal shelter, Mattie won't give up on either one of them. She signs papers agreeing to become Wesley's guardian, and you know she will get that little dog out, too.

Mattie Rigsbee is a metaphor for God and, in their relationships with her all throughout the story, the other characters experience what faith is like. Nobody experiences an escape clause, and nobody experiences a loophole. But they all experience being saved, which is an entirely different matter.

It can be easy to mistake faith for an escape clause because sometimes authentic faith can feel like an escape. Real faith can feel like being plucked from the jaws of disaster at the last minute. People who experience an adult conversion sometimes report their experience in such terms. One of the most famous conversions of the twentieth century was that of Thomas Merton, who lived what, for the 1930s at least, was a wild and undisciplined life, a life filled with booze, parties, sex, and smoking. When he was about sixteen years old, Merton fathered a child in England, which prompted his legal guardian to ship him off in disgrace to his relatives in the United States.[4]

Much later in life, after his conversion to Catholicism, and after many years as a Trappist monk, Merton wrote:

> Ultimately, faith is the only key to the universe. The final meaning of human existence, and the answers to questions on which all our happiness depends cannot be reached in any other way.[5]

For Merton, the experience of being "saved"—and the faith that came with this experience—changed everything. It was, indeed, like being snatched from the brink of disaster. It was an Escape. But it was not an escape clause, because there was no contract; there was only the Escape. Merton saw faith more as "the only key to the universe," not as an escape clause. It was not a matter of getting away with something; rather, it was more a getting away *from* something. To "have" authentic faith does not mean you can now ride through life in a spiritual Rolls Royce sipping a glass of spiritual champagne.

In a letter to a spiritual seeker, Merton wrote:

> That is my quarrel with religious people. They are selling answers and consolations. They are in the reassurance business. I give you no reassurance whatever except that I know your void and I am in it, but I have a different way of understanding myself in it. It is not that much more delightful. But it does to me make a great deal of sense–for me . . .[6]

Authentic faith is not a set of ready-made answers and consolations. That it is or may be reassuring at times is incidental. Rather, faith is a way to look at and understand life, the world, other people, the universe, and human existence. The result of faith is being able to make some sense of it all and find some meaning there. At its roots, faith is not a positive feeling, or a feeling of any kind, for that matter.

A "faith" that is an escape clause generally finds it necessary to condemn the world as evil, whereas authentic faith dedicates itself to serving and saving the world. Genuine faith embraces the world without pretending that there is no evil in the world. Father Godfrey Diekmann, the great Benedictine scholar and liturgist, once recalled his participation in discussions at the Second Vatican Council, in the mid-1960s, that produced the council's groundbreaking document on liturgical reform. The final words spoken by the priest at Mass are: "Go in peace to love and serve the Lord." Diekmann said that if he had it to do over again, he would recommend that the priest say, instead, "Go in peace to love and serve the world."[7]

If someone's faith becomes an escape clause or loophole, you may be sure that this faith is no longer the faith of a grown-up but the faith of someone who is emotionally and spiritually childish. Don't assume, however, that an escape clause or loophole faith is the same as a faith that continues to believe in miracles. Not by a long shot.

Italian director Ermanno Olmi's wonderful 1978 film, *The Tree of Wooden Clogs*, portrays a year in the life of a community of peasants in Northern Italy at the end of the nineteenth century. Film critic Leonard Maltin calls it a "simple, quietly beautiful epic; a work of art."[8] Throughout the film, Olmi portrays the Catholic faith of the poor community in ways that show it to be unsophisticated but healthy.

One day a family's cow becomes ill, so the widowed mother of the family sends for the veterinarian. When the vet arrives, he examines the cow, pronounces the condition hopeless, and advises the woman to butcher the cow so at least the family will have the meat. The woman is devastated, for her family is already practically destitute. Without the cow her children will have no milk. So the woman begins to pray to Jesus and to the Blessed Virgin, begging them to not let her cow die.

After the woman goes to the little village church to pray, she goes outside and fills a bottle with water from the little stream that runs by the church, praying as she does that God will bless the water. Returning home, the woman goes into the barn and pours the water down the cow's throat, praying all the while. Then she goes away and leaves the cow lying there in a sad condition.

Later in the day, two of the woman's children come running to tell her that the cow is standing. She runs to the barn and sure enough, the cow is well again, as healthy as ever. The woman kneels and says a prayer of thanksgiving, but it's almost as if she is not surprised by what has happened. The faith of this woman is such that she expects miracles. Does this mean her faith is an escape clause or loophole? By no means.

A faith that looks for and expects miracles can be a perfectly authentic adult faith. The difference between an escape-clause faith and a faith that is not surprised by miracles is that the latter does not view miracles—such as the cure of a sick cow upon which a poor family depends for food—as anything out of the ordinary. At the same time, real faith does not depend on miracles. Real faith does not vanish if miracles don't happen. If the woman's cow had not been cured, she would not have despaired or become an unbeliever.

The point here is that a miracle, big or small, is not an escape clause or loophole. Rather, a miracle is a "natural," as it were, consequence of authentic faith. Look at any miracle story in the Gospels—the story in the Gospel of Luke, for example, of the man who was blind:

> As [Jesus] approached Jericho, a blind man was sitting by the roadside begging. When he heard a crowd going by, he asked what was happening. They told him, "Jesus of Nazareth is passing by." Then he shouted, "Jesus, Son of David, have mercy on me!" Those who were in front sternly ordered him to be quiet; but he shouted even more loudly, "Son of David, have mercy on me!"
>
> Jesus stood still and ordered the man to be brought to him; and when he came near, he asked him, "What do you want me to do for you?" He said, "Lord, let me see again." Jesus said to him, "Receive your sight; your faith has saved you." Immediately he regained his sight and followed him, glorifying God; and all the people, when they saw it, praised God (18:35–43).

This is a more or less typical gospel account of a miraculous cure—typical because it has four parts. First, the afflicted person petitions Jesus to help him. Second, Jesus asks for more specific information: What, exactly, does the petitioner want? Third, the afflicted person states explicitly what he wants from Jesus. Fourth, Jesus tells the person that his or her *"faith has saved you."*

Notice that Jesus does not say, "Your faith has cured you." Perhaps even more remarkably, Jesus does not say, "*I* cure you." He says, "Your faith has *saved* you." For the Gospel of Luke, the point here is that a miraculous cure is but a sign of something much bigger. A miraculous cure is a sign that *salvation* has come to this person. The miracle is just a physical manifestation of a much deeper reality, the reality of salvation. Of course, this is appropriate because *salvation* means "healing and liberation for both this life and the next."

A miraculous cure is simply a sign that faith is real and active in a person's life and/or in the lives of those close to that person. Your faith "saves you," and one way faith sometimes "saves" a person is through a miraculous physical cure. So a miracle is both a sign and a manifestation of genuine faith. Such a faith has nothing to do with loopholes and escape clauses.

Of course, faith "saves," but—as mentioned above—the "saving" faith does is best understood as spiritual healing and liberation that begins in this life and comes to completion in the next. It is the spiritual character of salvation that makes it what it is, but because we humans are embodied spirits, there is nothing that affects us spiritually that does not affect us physically as well. Sometimes a person's experience of this faith that saves is such that—at some point in his or her lifetime—it includes physical, psychological, or emotional healing, too.

But is this not beginning to sound suspiciously like an escape clause or loophole in the unpredictable contract called "life"? Here we have this person like any other person, but because he or she has faith, then sometimes, at least, a miraculous cure—whether physical or emotional—comes with the package. Is that not an escape? A wriggling out of the darkness an unbeliever would need to face head-on? On the contrary—because the healing that faith sometimes brings is not magic but a "natural" consequence of faith.

In the technical sense, magic is the power to manipulate or control supernatural forces by the use of certain words and/or gestures. In magic, the human person has power over the supernatural, can make supernatural forces do what he or she wants them to do by using the right formulaic words and/or gestures. In faith, however, there is no power to control God or to force God to do anything. Returning to the example of the widowed woman in *The Tree of Wooden Clogs*, it may look at first glance like she controls, or is trying to control, God by saying certain prayers and by giving the cow holy water to drink, thereby causing the animal to be cured. Rather, the woman's prayers are petitions for divine favor, and the holy water is simply the woman's Catholic sacramental imagination at work. In other words, because the woman knows that God's love is present and active in all created things, she expresses her faith by collecting the holy water and giving it to the cow to drink. She attributes no magical power either to her prayers or to the water. Because she is Catholic, she expresses her faith by the use of created things, for example, the blessed water. She says her prayers and leaves the situation entirely with God, believing that whatever happens will be for the best, that God will be with her and her children whether the cow lives or dies.

Had the cow died instead of being cured, the woman's faith would not have been weakened but strengthened, just as it was because the cow was cured. This woman's faith is no escape clause or loophole because she does not think of her faith as a way to wiggle out of anything. Rather, her faith is complete trust in God's loving compassion regardless of what happens. Faith is not magic because faith is no way to control God or force God to do anything.

What about Catholic beliefs concerning the afterlife, whatever it is that happens following death? It's easy to slip into simpleminded images of a heaven filled with billowy clouds, people in white robes playing harps, and winged angels floating about. Just as we depend on metaphors and analogies to talk about transcendent realities in this life, so we must do the same in order to talk about the mystery of the afterlife. The traditional terms are "heaven" and "hell," two words used to express the belief that there are connections between this life and the next, specifically between choices we make in this life and the condition we can expect in the next life.

Again, it is important to remember that human language and human concepts are extremely limited when it comes to talking about matters that leave the human intellect in the dust. "Heaven" and "hell" are simply words we use to talk about conditions following death that are Good and Bad. We also use these words to carry our understanding that our behavior in this life will have consequences, Good or Bad, in the next. Of course, this leads us down the paths trod by moral theology and ethics, and we have neither the space nor the inclination to get involved in this particular line of thought.

Perhaps it is sufficient to keep in mind Catholicism's conviction that even in this life we begin to share in the life of heaven. It's not as if there is a complete break between our condition "here" and the condition we will be in "there." As the *Catechism of the Catholic Church* explains:

> When the Church prays "our Father who art in heaven," she is professing that we are the People of God, already seated "with him in the heavenly places in Christ Jesus" and "hidden with Christ in God" [Eph 26; Col 3:3]; yet at the same time, "here indeed we groan, and long to put on our heavenly dwelling" [2 Cor 5:2; cf. Phil 3:20; Heb 13:14].[9]

The traditional belief that both Good and Bad conditions are possible following death means that Christianity is not about an automatic ticket to heaven; that authentic Christian faith is not a cosmic loophole. Rather, God creates us free, we have choices that we cannot sidestep, and the ways we make those choices have eternal implications. If we act on faith, however—in fidelity to our relationship with Christ—then we need have no anxiety about our eternal destiny. And in the end, faith is about depending on our relationship with a God who is infinitely forgiving and merciful.

As we saw in an earlier chapter, the best argument against any inadequate understanding of faith is the faith of Jesus in the Gospels. Time and again, in the Gospels, Jesus' faith is no escape clause or loophole. It does not protect him but, rather, compels him to remain faithful to his mission in spite of the dangers of doing so. It was faith that kept Jesus true to his task, even to the point of terrible suffering and the most ignominious, painful death. But, you may wonder, must we not say that ultimately Jesus' faith was an escape clause because his Resurrection was the ultimate escape?

We could speak of Jesus' faith as the ultimate escape clause only if his faith had saved him from experiencing death at all. But the Gospels make it clear that Jesus experienced death absolutely. After he died on the cross, Jesus was as dead as any human being can be. So his faith offered no escape from the ultimate experience of human limitation and finitude. Only after he passed through death's dark doors did Jesus experience resurrection—a mystery the Gospels do not clarify but only describe in terms of its effects on Jesus as he was present among his disciples following his Resurrection.

The faith of Jesus was no escape clause, and our faith is no escape clause. Rather, faith is the source of courage and trust in the face of death, and sometimes faith compels us to stand up for what's right, even when the consequence may be suffering and even death. Rather than being a loophole, faith is the source of a vision that transcends this life, a perspective that can take more than this life into account, a perception that there is more to life than just what meets the eye.

Faith is no loophole or escape clause. Instead, faith leads you along a way of trust, but not blind trust. Rather, faith leads you to trust in your own deepest intuitions and take your most significant experiences of meaning and love as indications that Meaning and Love are the final answer to all of life's most perplexing questions. Rather than being an escape clause, faith is ultimately an experience of Meaning in the midst of meaninglessness, Light in the deepest darkness, and Love in the face of the most inhuman manifestations of hatred and cruelty.

As he so often does, G. K. Chesterton provides words that clarify exactly what we mean: "Faith is always at a disadvantage; it is a perpetually defeated thing which survives all its conquerors." And: "This is the definition of a faith. A faith is that which is able to survive a mood."[10]

More often than not, it is a mood that inclines us to act as if faith should be an escape clause or loophole. Yet, we live in a culture that takes moods with utmost seriousness. A dictionary defines *mood* as "a state of mind or emotion," and the dominant culture takes emotions with utmost seriousness, as if nothing is more real than an emotion. Yet, as Chesterton saw, an authentic faith, a grown-up faith, is that which is able to survive an emotion. Faith is deeper and stronger that any emotion or mood. It is even possible—a little sarcasm, here—that faith may lead you to act in a way contrary to your mood, your emotion, how you are feeling at the moment!

The startling thing is that when you act according to faith, rather than according to a mood or emotion, in the long run you will find peace that surpasses understanding. Ah, you may wonder, but is it not possible that faith and a mood may coincide? Possible, yes. But we can't afford to automatically presume that faith and emotion do coincide in a given situation. We need to be more careful and self-critical than that. If anything, we should begin with the contrary assumption that faith and feeling do *not* coincide. That is the more difficult, more narrow path, and the path that is more likely to lead along the ways of the gospel. The ultimate test is whether acting contrary to your mood leads to peace on down the line, a few days or weeks later—and it takes faith to be patient, to wait and see.

Some words of the modern spiritual master Carlo Carretto (1910–1988) illustrate the point:

> Do you want to know the secret of true happiness? Of deep and genuine peace? Do you want to solve at a blow all your difficulties in relations with your neighbor, bring all polemic to an end, avoid all dissension?
>
> Well, decide here and now to love things and men as Jesus loved them, that is, to the point of self-sacrifice. Do not bother with the bookkeeping of love; love without keeping accounts.
>
> If you know someone who is decent and likeable, love him, but if someone else is very unlikable, love him just the same. If someone greets you and smiles, greet him and smile back, but if someone else treads on your feet, smile just the same. If someone does you a good turn, thank the Lord for it, but if someone else slanders you, persecutes you, curses you, strikes you, thank him and carry on.
>
> Do not say, "I'm right, he's wrong." Say: "I must love him as myself." This is the kind of love Jesus taught: a love that transforms, vivifies, enriches, brings peace.[11]

See the trouble you can get yourself into if mood or emotion is your constant guide? When we identify the way of faith with the way a mood or emotion tells us to go, we turn faith into an escape clause or loophole, a mere justification for what we feel like doing, an excuse for doing what we feel like doing. If a loved one does something that irritates you, it's good to let him or her know that. But if the irritating behavior continues due to your friend's simple absentmindedness or lack of self-awareness, there comes a point where faith leads you to clam up and simply love your neighbor as yourself. But you do need to love yourself, for authentic faith requires you to accept life as a gift and to cultivate life within yourself.

An escape-clause or loophole faith is, in fact, no faith at all but a cheap substitute that merely allows you to follow your own inclinations instead of being guided by your intimacy with the Risen Christ and by the spirit of the gospel. The peace that a loophole or escape-clause faith gives is fleeting and soon vanishes with the moment, while authentic faith may not feel good for the moment but soon gives a peace that nothing in this world can give, a peace that lasts beyond time and space.

Faith is not a crutch

One of the most common charges leveled at religious faith is that it is nothing but a crutch for people too weak to stand up and face life directly. "Religion is fine for those who need a crutch to get through life." Nothing could be further from the truth, of course, not as far as authentic faith is concerned.

The full truth is that both faith and the choice to live without faith can be crutches. For some people faith—or rather an immature form of faith—is, in fact, a crutch. But for some people, the choice to live without faith is also a crutch. In both cases, you're talking about people who are unwilling to stand up and live life on their own two feet. Some use religion as a crutch, some use agnosticism, atheism, religious indifference, or skepticism as a crutch. Any of these can be a crutch, and any of them can be an honest position of courage. To want nothing to do with religion or to say that religion is nothing but a crutch for the weak is to overlook the fact that any life stance or worldview can be used as a crutch. The difference comes in how you understand and relate to your religion or to your agnosticism, skepticism, and so on.

If your religion or your agnosticism is a challenging presence in your life that inspires you to take risks and to continue to grow, it is no crutch. If your religion or agnosticism or religious indifference supports a life position of smug superiority or abject helplessness, it is a crutch. In other words, for unbelievers to accuse believers of needing a "crutch" is disingenuous, at best. Any worldview or outlook on life can be a crutch if you use it to protect yourself from reality.

That's one perspective. Another might be to say that, well, some people have no choice but to use a crutch to get around. Without the crutch they would not be able to move about at all. If a person has a broken leg or a sprained ankle, for example, he or she needs a crutch, and who is going to deny that person the use of a crutch? Some people need to use a crutch or set of crutches all the time because they have some disability. Anyone who says that people who need to use crutches are weaklings is insensitive and unrealistic, to say the least.

Some—perhaps many—people may use faith as a spiritual crutch, a way to help them get around in the world, because they have no choice in the matter. Their spiritual or emotional handicaps make this necessary. If this is the case, it certainly does not mean that these people's faith is inauthentic. All it means is that the crutch metaphor has serious limitations. A crutch is a means of support to compensate for a natural means of support—such as a leg or ankle—that, for whatever reason, has been weakened.

In this sense, it may not be fair to accuse religion of being a crutch for those unable to stand up and face life on their own two feet. In fact, most people are unable to face life with no assistance at all. For most people, it's more a question of where they choose to get their help. The question is whether you choose to get support from a source that enslaves or a source that liberates, a source that limits your view or one that broadens your horizons. Many people rely on addictions for support, addictions to everything from food to alcohol to nicotine, from an endless search for total economic security to television watching.

The difference between all these and authentic religious faith is that faith, if it is real, is a source of security only by paradox. Faith gives security by leading you to give up security. Faith offers reassurance by helping you to give up a need for reassurance. Faith becomes a safety net only when you step into the void. Faith gives certainty only when you are willing to live with uncertainty. Faith is a crutch only if you stand up and walk with no visible means of support.

If the Christian life has a manifesto it would be the Sermon on the Mount in the Gospel of Matthew, and if the Sermon on the

Mount has a heart, it would be the Beatitudes. Take a look at the Beatitudes and ask yourself how anyone could accuse a religion, one that asks you to base your life on the following ideals, of being a crutch:

> When Jesus saw the crowds, he went up the mountain; and after he sat down, his disciples came to him. Then he began to speak, and taught them, saying:
> "Blessed are the poor in spirit, for theirs is the kingdom of heaven.
> "Blessed are those who mourn, for they will be comforted.
> "Blessed are the meek, for they will inherit the earth.
> "Blessed are those who hunger and thirst for righteousness, for they will be filled.
> "Blessed are the merciful, for they will receive mercy.
> "Blessed are the pure in heart, for they will see God.
> "Blessed are the peacemakers, for they will be called children of God.
> "Blessed are those who are persecuted for righteousness' sake, for theirs is the kingdom of heaven.
> "Blessed are you when people revile you and persecute you and utter all kinds of evil against you falsely on my account. Rejoice and be glad, for your reward is great in heaven, for in the same way they persecuted the prophets who were before you" (5:1–12).

The gospel of Jesus asks you to embrace a way of life that will get you considerable inconvenience, to say the least. And critics call this a crutch? That isn't a crutch critics see, it's a cross, and a cross is to carry, a burden, not a means of support for the weak of knee.

Where does the accusation come from that religion is nothing but a crutch for those too weak to face life directly? As we observed above, it is quite possible to use religion as a crutch in a negative sense. Plenty of people use religion as an excuse to avoid taking risks instead of allowing it to do its real job, which is to make risk-takers out of us, big-time. Consider some familiar words of St. Paul:

> Let the same mind be in you that was in Christ Jesus, who, though he was in the form of God, did not regard equality with God as something to be exploited, but emptied himself, taking the form of a slave, being born in human likeness. And being found in human form, he humbled himself and became obedient to the point of death—even death on a cross. Therefore God also highly exalted him and gave him the name that is above every name, so that at the name of Jesus every knee should bend, in heaven and on earth and under the earth, and every tongue should confess that Jesus Christ is Lord, to the glory of God the Father.
>
> Therefore, my beloved, just as you have always obeyed me, not only in my presence, but much more now in my absence, work out your own salvation with fear and trembling; for it is God who is at work in you, enabling you both to will and to work for his good pleasure (Philippians 2:5–13).

We might call this St. Paul's theology of faith in a nutshell. For Paul, faith means living out an "imitation of Christ," that is, being in the world the way Christ was in the world, having the mind of Christ in the world here and now. The key words in the passage from Philippians are "emptied," "humbled," and "obedient." In effect, Paul tells his readers that faith means to "empty" yourself in service to God and others, to "humble" yourself in a world that admires self-glorification, and "obey" God's will for you.

Does this sound like faith is a crutch? Not likely. Although some people may use faith, inappropriately, as a crutch, a faith that is truly a crutch isn't truly faith at all but a distortion of faith that ends up being its own handicap. When faith becomes a crutch, it hobbles and restricts rather than heals and liberates, as it is meant to do. When faith becomes a crutch, it slows you down and keeps you spiritually childish; when faith is authentic, it nourishes spiritual adulthood.

One of the greatest spiritual classics of all time is a book that has a reputation for being the most widely read book in the world, after the Bible. *The Imitation of Christ* was written by Thomas à Kempis, an early fifteenth-century author who lived in the Netherlands and belonged to the Brethren of the Common Life, a group that promoted a deep devotional life among Christians. In *The Imitation of Christ,* Chapter 23 ("Four Things That Bring Great Peace"), you will find the following words, and the author has Jesus speak them to the reader. Notice how clearly this passage echoes Scripture:

> Always strive . . . to do another's will rather than your own [see Matthew 26:39]. Always choose to have less rather than more [see Matthew 10:10]. Always seek the lowest place [see Luke 14:10] and be submissive in all things. Always desire and pray that God's will be entirely fulfilled in you [see Matthew 6:10].[1]

We need to be careful to not misinterpret the *Imitation's* words about seeking the lowest place and being submissive, of course. Faith is no crutch, but authentic faith also does not turn people into doormats for others to walk all over, all for the sake of a heavenly reward. Faith is never Karl Marx's "opiate of the masses" by a far cry. When the *Imitation* urges the reader to seek the lowest place and be submissive, it is talking about a kind of spiritual assertiveness, in fact. It takes true humility to take big risks for the sake of truth and justice; it takes someone who is truly submissive to the gospel, someone who is willing to suffer the consequences of standing up for what's right.

The quotation above from *The Imitation of Christ* is a thumbnail description of what authentic faith looks like, or how authentic faith behaves. Do these words sound like the description of a crutch? Rather, if these words about faith are accurate they describe a life of constant struggle against being self-centered—of a wildly countercultural existence in a world that encourages being self-centered at every turn. The faith that *The Imitation of Christ* takes for granted is no crutch.

Here is the faith of *The Imitation of Christ*:

> It is vanity to seek riches that are sure to perish and to put your hope in them [see Ecclesiastes 5:9]. It is vanity to pursue honors and to set yourself up on a pedestal. . . . It is vanity to wish for a long life and to care little about leading a good life. It is vanity to give thought only to this present life and not to think of the one to come. It is vanity to love what is transitory and not to hasten to where everlasting joy

abides. Keep this proverb often in mind: *The eye is not sat-
isfied with seeing, nor the ear filled with hearing* [Ecclesiastes
1:8].[2]

Faith, for *The Imitation of Christ*, is no crutch but a source of
growth toward full human maturity. It is only a grown-up who can
follow the words just quoted here. It is only someone who is spiritually adult who can read these words and agree that they are worth following as an ideal. The point is not that you must be able to keep
these ideals perfectly. Few ever do that. The point is that if you can
read these words and take them to heart as ideals worth striving for
over a lifetime, then you know what authentic faith is, and you know
that faith is no mere crutch.

Can you see, reading these words from the *Imitation*, how utterly
countercultural they are? Can you see what a huge conflict there is
between these words and the ideals that the dominant culture hugs to
its breast? It is so obvious. All you need do is pluck the latest issue of
People from a magazine rack and flip through its pages to see that the
people the dominant culture admires are not people who believe that
"it is vanity to seek riches that are sure to perish and to put your hope
in them." They are not people who believe that "it is vanity to pursue
honors and to set yourself up on a pedestal."

Quite the opposite! Authentic Christian faith is no crutch for the
weak but a way of being in the world that, if you take it seriously, is
likely to make you a person with little interest in the nonsense that fills
the heart and mind of the dominant popular culture. Faith turns you
into a person who cares little for appearances and less for what's popular. Faith turns you into a person who values, above all things, a
warm and lively relationship with God and with other people in this
world. Faith isn't a crutch; rather, it's an ongoing and mysterious
source of life to the full.

As an aside, we might say that faith isn't a crutch, it's a *clutch*.
Here is a dictionary's definition of a *clutch*: "Any of various devices for
engaging and disengaging two working parts of a shaft or of a shaft
and a driving mechanism." As a metaphor for faith, "clutch" isn't bad.
If faith is a clutch, its function is to engage us with God and disengage
us from whatever comes between us and God.

One of the most remarkable facts about true faith is the extent to
which it is not a crutch. Rather than being something to lean on, faith

leads you to stand up on your own two feet and step out each day to engage the world—not on the world's terms, however, but on Christ's terms. If there is anything that characterizes a faith that becomes a crutch, it is its tendency to become a source of phoniness. Well might we attend to the words of the anonymous author of the fourteenth-century spiritual classic, *The Cloud of Unknowing*. What he says about contemplative prayer might as easily be applied to faith in general:

> The spiritual and physical comportment of those involved in any sort of pseudo-contemplation is apt to appear very eccentric, whereas God's friends always bear themselves with simple grace. Anyone noticing these deluded folk at prayer might see strange things indeed! If their eyes are open, they are apt to be staring blankly like a madman or peering like one who saw the devil, and well they might, for he is not far off. Sometimes their eyes look like the eyes of wounded sheep near death. Some will let their heads droop to one side, as if a worm were in their ears . . . . They are usually hypocrites."[3]

When faith becomes a crutch—as it does if we are not on guard—it becomes a source of spiritual phoniness and religious hypocrisy. Instead of being a source of ongoing healing and liberation, it becomes something merely to lean on, something to get you through the night. Faith is full of patience, courage, and long-suffering, and faith inclines you to leap into the darkness. Faith is no excuse for anything.

Sometimes even simple stories of faith can be highly instructive if we want a better understanding of what faith is and is not. Take, for example, the famous story of St. Francis of Assisi and the Wolf of Gubbio. This story is from the fourteenth-century classic, *The Little Flowers of Saint Francis.*[4] Largely fanciful tales with historical connections that are tenuous, at best, nevertheless these often delightful stories teach valuable lessons about the nature of authentic faith and how to recognize it.

In the account of the encounter between St. Francis and the ravenous wolf, the narrator tells us that the wolf "had devoured not only animals but men and women too, so much that it held all the people in such terror that they all went armed whenever they went into the country-side as if they were off to grim war."[5]

Saint Francis happened to be in Gubbio when fear of the wolf was at its highest:

> In pity for them [St. Francis] made arrangements to go out and meet the wolf. "Have care, Brother Francis, not to go outside the gate," they said, "because the wolf who has devoured many will surely kill you." But Francis, hoping in the Lord Jesus Christ who rules the spirits of all flesh, without the protection of shield or helmet, but guarding himself with the Sign of the Holy Cross, went out of the gate with a companion, putting all his trust in the Lord who makes all who believe in him "walk without harm over viper and asp, but tread not only on the wolf, but on the lion too and the serpent."[6]

Out Francis goes "fearlessly" to meet the terrible wolf, many people watching from behind the walls of the city to see what will happen. Immediately the wolf runs out snarling to meet Francis and his companion. But the only weapon Francis has to defend himself is "the Sign of the Cross."

> The blessed father met him with the Sign of the Cross, and by divine strength restrained the wolf from himself and his companion, checked its charge and closed his cruelly open mouth. Calling him then, he said, "Come to me, brother wolf, and in Christ's name I command you not to harm me or anybody." It is wondrous that one Sign of the Cross closed that awful maw. As soon as the order was given, like a lamb and not a wolf, with lowered head he laid himself at the feet of the saint.[7]

Francis then delivers a short homily to the wolf, gently admonishing the animal, telling him that for all the killing he has done and the terror he has inspired, he deserves to die himself, "to be hacked like any footpad or loathly murderer."[8] The people have every right to hate the wolf, Francis says. All the same, Francis tells the wolf, he wants the wolf and the people to make peace with one another.

The wolf, by movements of head and tail, shows St. Francis that he promises to live at peace and is ready to return with Francis to

Gubbio to present himself to the people in a spirit of forgiveness and reconciliation. Once back in the city square, Francis preaches a sermon:

> It was, he said, because of their sins that such scourges were allowed; and how much more perilous was the flames of Gehenna's fire which can devour the damned for ever, than the ravening of a wolf which can kill only the body; and how terrible it was to be plunged into the jaws of hell when one poor animal could hold so huge a crowd in panic and peril. "Return, therefore, dear friends, to the Lord and do proper penance, and God will free you from the wolf now, and in the future from the pit of consuming fire. Listen, dear folk, for brother wolf who is present here has promised me and pledged his word to make peace with you, to do no one harm if you promise to give him his daily necessities. And on his behalf I promise and pledge to you that he will faithfully observe the ways of peace." Then all there gathered and with a mighty shout promised to feed the wolf for ever. And Saint Francis said to the wolf before them all: "And to you, brother wolf, promise to keep faith with them, and do harm to neither man nor beast?" The wolf knelt and bowed his head, and with conciliatory movements of body, tail and ears, indicated that he would keep his promise.[9]

The wolf then spends the rest of his life living peacefully in Gubbio, and not even the dogs bark at him. Eventually, he grows old and dies, and the people of Gubbio mourn his passing as they would a dear friend, for the wolf always reminded them of St. Francis and his miraculous visit to Gubbio.

Notice that in this story the faith of St. Francis is in no sense a crutch to support him in his weakness. Rather, faith is a source of boldness and courage in the face of danger. Francis tells the people of Gubbio, in effect, that the reason they have been ruled by fear is their lack of faith.

One reason the story of St. Francis and the Wolf of Gubbio has been so popular for so many centuries is that it stands so clearly as a metaphor for what most people experience as the central struggle of faith. The wolf is a metaphor for everything that threatens faith, all the fears and anxieties and doubts that assail the believer and try to attract him or her to give up on faith and rely on other, more tangible but, in truth, less reliable forms of security. Saint Francis, of course, is a metaphor for authentic faith, a faith that looks danger in the eye and tames it by trust in God.

In the story, and in the experience of countless Christians through the centuries, authentic faith tames our fears and anxieties, rendering them harmless. So faith does not function as a crutch but as a source of courage, humility, patience, and trust. Faith doesn't make you run away from your fears anymore than faith made St. Francis run away from the wolf. Rather, faith leads you to face your fears and anxieties and tame them, just as Francis tamed the ravenous wolf of Gubbio.

In his sermon, Francis tells the citizens of Gubbio that if they had relied on their faith instead of on weapons of various kinds, they, too, could have tamed the wolf. Not only that, but he explains that the wolf—that is, their fears and anxieties—will remain among them, and they must befriend the wolf as their part of the deal. The wolf remains harmless as long as the people care for him.

In other words, faith doesn't make our fears and anxieties go away. Rather, faith acknowledges the presence of fear and anxiety. Indeed, faith even shows care and respect for fear and anxiety, and allows them to live and go about their business. But faith renders fear and anxiety harmless; it tames them, precisely by acknowledging their presence. For *faith can only be true to itself because fear and anxiety exist.* Faith needs fear and anxiety, otherwise there is no reason for faith to exist. Just as darkness and light need each other in order to exist, so faith and fear need each other in order to be what each one is.

Faith is not the solution to all problems

Consider the following words from St. Paul:

> . . . if you confess with your lips that Jesus is Lord and believe in your heart that God raised him from the dead, you will be saved. For one believes with the heart and so is justified, and one confesses with the mouth and so is saved" (Romans 10:9–10).

A good many sincere people believe that they can solve life's problems by a sincere verbal confession of faith in Christ. Would that the mystery of salvation were so simple! But actual human experience tells us otherwise. It's easy to overlook the future tense in St. Paul's words. He says that we "*will be* saved," and his other key words are "believes" and "confesses," which are active, not past definite, verbs. Saint Paul's understanding of salvation is about a lifelong *process*, not an event that is accomplished once and for all in a moment. If you "confess with your lips" and "believe in your heart" *day after day, month after month, year after year,* ultimately you "*will be*" saved.

Salvation, in Paul's theology, is never once-and-for-all. Rather, salvation, like the kingdom, or reign, of God is "already but not yet." Salvation is at work in us, but it is never fully accomplished in time and space, in this world. No one can say, "I'm saved." The most anyone can say is, "I'm being saved." Keep in mind, too, that *salvation* is a word easy to misunderstand. Salvation isn't only about what happens to us after we die. Rather, salvation might best be translated as "spiritual healing and liberation," a process that begins, and that we experience, here and now, in this life. Salvation—spiritual healing and liberation—begins here and now but is fully accomplished only on the other side of dusty death.

All this means that we can never understand faith as the solution to all our problems and difficulties. Rather, faith becomes the source we draw upon when we cope with our problems and difficulties. Faith doesn't make problems and difficulties go away; rather, it helps us have the patience, courage, fortitude, and persistence to face our problems and difficulties and work through them. Faith helps you to see that the cross—whatever form(s) it takes in your life—far from being meaningless, is your share in the mystery of salvation, not only for you but for all those you love and, ultimately, for the entire world.

Citizens of the so-called "developed" Western nations tend to have a remarkable attitude toward not only physical pain but toward difficulties, troubles, anxiety, anguish, stress— anything unpleasant that you can imagine. The dominant culture encourages us to do whatever is necessary to make anxiety, troubles, or stress go away. Got a headache, heartburn, sore muscle, stomachache, tired eyes? The shelves of the supermarket or drugstore groan with their burden of remedies—pills, syrups, ointments—all bearing the promise to return you to a discomfort-free life. Swallow that pill, slurp that syrup, rub that ointment into your skin, and relief will belong to you.

Trouble is, we tend to transfer this attitude to our spirituality, which is when we slip into thinking of faith as a remedy for the troubles and woes that aspirin and antacid can do nothing about. People who think of faith as the ultimate solution to all difficulties miss the point. Life's troubles and woes bring us smack up against the mysterious nature of life. If anything, faith intensifies the mystery, or makes us more sensitive to the mystery, rather than making it all seem crystal clear. Saint Teresa of Avila, the sixteenth-century Spanish Carmelite mystic, was an all-around practical woman. She is famous for her remark to God, in the midst of all her efforts to reform the Carmelite Order, and the resistance she encountered from many sides, that if this is how God treats his friends, it's no wonder that he has so few of them.

In other words, if anything, faith is likely to increase your troubles rather than decrease them. Faith is a light that tends to lead you in directions you would not otherwise go. Sometimes those directions are along paths that are anything but smooth and easy. Faith tends to lead you in directions that heighten your insecurity rather than lower it. Look at some of the most obvious examples of how faith works, examples such as the saints. Heroic faith leads a person to a high-risk life, a life where troubles and woes are commonplace in everyday life. Take someone from our own era, Dorothy Day (1897–1980), co-founder of the Catholic Worker Movement, which is dedicated to social justice, service to the poor, and pacifism. Enthusiastic about Communism during the early 1900s, Day was arrested during a woman's suffrage demonstration in 1917 and was an ardent pacifist during World War I. Along the way, she underwent an abortion, then later lived with a man and bore his child. Gradually, she gravitated toward the Catholic Church and in 1927, after she became a Catholic and had her daughter baptized as well, she left the man she was living with. In 1932 she met Peter Maurin, an older man whose Catholic ideals for social justice fired her imagination, and together they began publishing a little newspaper, *The Catholic Worker*, which they sold for a penny a copy.

With Peter Maurin, her idealistic friend and mentor, Dorothy Day founded the first Catholic Worker house of hospitality in 1935, dedicated to helping the needy—a mission that lasted until her death in 1980 and continues to go on at Catholic Worker houses of hospitality in various cities across the United States.

Dorothy Day's faith led her to wear second-hand clothing for most of her adult life, to live with the poor and the unpleasant, to eat meals concocted of the most amazing variety of ingredients tossed together into a pot and called "soup." Here is one of the ways Dorothy Day described her life in her autobiography, *The Long Loneliness*:

> As I write this there is less than a hundred dollars in the
> bank, the line of men stretches to the corner, and our
> households here and at Maryfarm and Peter Maurin farm
> comprise seventy-five people or more. How can we go on?
> We are as sure as we ever were that God can multiply the
> loaves, as He has sheltered the homeless these many years.[1]

Of course, most of us are not called to live the kind of life
Dorothy Day lived. But the point is that authentic faith is never pure-
ly a constant source of comfort and consolation, a solution to every
problem or anxiety that comes along. Yes, faith can and should be a
source of consolation. But authentic faith is also a source of something
else. Sometimes authentic faith is a pain in the derriére. To adapt
Dostoyevsky's famous saying about love, from *The Brothers
Karamazov:* Active faith in reality can be a harsh and dreadful thing
compared to faith in dreams.

In a way, the inclination to think of faith as a solution to troubles
and worries places us in the middle of a debate that goes back to the
sixteenth century and the Protestant Reformation. One of the key
points of contention between the Protestant Reformers and the
Catholic Church was whether or not faith requires good works. The
Council of Trent (1545–1563)—Catholicism's response to the
Protestant Reformation—understood the Protestant position to advo-
cate a faith minus good works. The Council of Trent's response
emphasized that a faith that trusts in God alone is an incomplete faith.
Rather, faith "also requires our good works and our mind's clinging to
God through belief in the doctrines proposed to us in Scripture and
in the Church's tradition."[2]

Rather than being a solution to all your problems, faith is likely
to increase your problems! Yes, faith helps you to focus on the essen-
tials of life and disregard the nonessentials and, in that sense, it light-
ens life's burdens. But at the same time, a life rooted in authentic
faith is a life familiar with insecurity, a life constantly lived on the
precipice, hovering over the void, characterized as much by uncertainty as certainty. There is no human life completely devoid of troubles and difficulties, hassles and grief—and a life based on authentic
faith will have more than most because it is a life based on trust in an
invisible God who is love, to be sure, but whose ways are unpredictable.

One of the pitfalls of relying too heavily on official church teachings is that it short-circuits God's unpredictability and absolute transcendence. The result is that there is, in effect, no longer any uncertainty, no longer any doubt. If you want to know exactly what God wants, what God's will is, simply attend to official doctrines and church teachings and obey all of them to the letter. This way you will find blessed relief from the most significant doubts and questions you may have.

The only trouble with this species of faith-as-solution-to-all-problems is that it depends upon the assumption that church teachings automatically carry infallibility, which means that the teaching becomes an absolute. Catholic doctrine teaches that the pope teaches infallibly only under very limited circumstances; in fact, this doctrine has been invoked only once since it was defined in 1870, to declare infallible the doctrine of the Assumption of the Blessed Virgin Mary into heaven, body and soul.

Unfortunately, the infallibility doctrine has led to what some have called "creeping infallibility," the impression that just about anything the pope says becomes infallible. This is a problem, because God is the only absolute, and no human conceptualization of God or of God's mind on a particular issue or topic can present that mystery to us all tied up with a neat little bow. All church teachings present an incomplete or partial statement of some truth. No human concept or idea can carry the whole truth. Therefore, while faith accepts and respects a given church teaching, authentic faith also understands that there is always more to be said, more of the truth to "unpack" from human experience of the divine. Therefore, there will always be questions, and there will always be doubts—which is okay.

To take a given church teaching as a complete and adequate statement of God's mind on a given issue or topic is to skip dangerously close to that good old human inclination: idol worship. Dress up a false god in holy raiment, and much of the time we'll go for it in a blink. Authentic faith, however, the faith those who are spiritually grown up try to cultivate, includes a healthy dose of iconoclasm, the readiness to destroy any finite object or idea that would present itself as an absolute. Authentic faith tries valiantly to relate to God alone as God, is wary of anything finite, anything limited, anything the human mind can grasp that would take the place of the true God. Official church teachings have much value, of course, and are necessary, but we need to guard against any tendency for such teachings to become church—rather than Christ-centered.

When anyone says in a particular situation or set of circumstances that he or she knows exactly what God wants or exactly what God thinks or exactly what God's will is, red flags go up all over the place for a faith that is authentic. Authentic faith insists on living with questions, insists on living with doubts, insists on living with uncertainty. Therefore, any faith that would offer answers to all questions, solutions to all problems, a doubt-free existence, and complete certainty about all that matters most in life is as phony as it can be, an idol, a false god, and really hardly faith at all.

It is also true that authentic faith is far from being antinomian—dead set against rules, laws, and regulations. Faith wants nothing to do with the anarchy that results when there are no rules, no laws, no official guidelines. As far as faith is concerned, ethics and morality—for example—cannot be separated from the personal, subjective dimension. Traditional Catholic moral theology has always taught that the individual ultimately must follow his or her well-informed conscience, and obviously we must include Christian doctrines and the teachings of the Church in forming our conscience. What, exactly, does this mean? Once again we find ourselves facing the existence of differing liberal and conservative interpretations of this idea in the Church today. Conservative Catholics tend to say that there is virtually no difference between a well-informed conscience and official church teachings. Liberal Catholics allow for a conscience that would require dissent from official teachings based on input from sources other than official church teachings, including the writings of theologians and other scholars.

Catholicism's understanding of divine revelation is a good example of how broad-minded it is. We don't limit revelation to the Scriptures; rather, we believe that revelation happens in the conjunction between Scripture and Sacred Tradition, one expression of which is the doctrines and official teachings of the Church.

Faith, for Catholicism, is no solution to all problems. But faith also does not leave you entirely to your own resources in a cold and indifferent world. Rather, faith is never a private, individual matter. Faith does not isolate you. Faith, by being exactly what it is, situates you in the midst of a *community* of faith so that you benefit from the collective wisdom of the community of faith, the Church. We find one expression of this collective wisdom in the doctrines and, yes, the laws, rules, and regulations of the Church.

Authentic faith neither obeys these laws and rules blindly—the ultra-conservative position—nor does it ignore them as completely irrelevant—the ultra-liberal position. Faith perceives in the laws and other legal paraphernalia of the Church, as well as in its moral and ethical prescriptions and guidelines, the wisdom of two thousand years of Christian experience informed and guided by the Holy Spirit. Nevertheless, in a given set of circumstances, those circumstances also figure into the equation. Unique conditions and circumstances in the lives of unique individuals matter, and the Holy Spirit is involved in these conditions and circumstances as well.

The truth is that the Church's official system of laws—called "canon law"—is meant to free, not restrict. Take, for example, the basic question of who is a Catholic and who is not. Sometimes Catholics who are quite observant about their religion are inclined to say that if you never attend Mass, you're not a Catholic. The Code of Canon Law is much more liberal and forgiving than that. It says that anyone who is baptized a Catholic remains a Catholic unless he or she formally renounces the Christian faith.[3] This is about as minimalistic as you can get!

Faith does not offer guaranteed solutions to all problems and issues, not even in the laws and rules of the Church. But it does provide a deep well from which to draw insight and guidance, a light in what could otherwise be a much darker and more confusing pilgrimage through life.

Another way in which people sometimes think of faith as a solution to problems is in the context of their personal relationships with others, whether family members, friends, or others with whom interaction frequently leads to conflict. One of the best examples of this is in the case of parents whose grown offspring choose to distance themselves from the Catholic faith. Sometimes such parents wonder why their faith does not help them bring their children back to the Church.

This is, without question, an issue that results in considerable anguish and heartache. Parents for whom the Catholic faith is central, who could not imagine living as anything but Catholics, naturally feel deep pain and disappointment when one or more of their grown children abandon the faith. Some marry outside the Church; others marry someone who belongs to a Protestant church or a non-Christian religion. Still others live a life of religious indifference. Choices such as these are naturally a source of much anguish to parents. "Why doesn't God bring my grown child back to the Church?"

This question assumes that faith should be a solution to a problem, a way to rid oneself of a source of pain and anguish. But this is to misunderstand the nature of faith. It is not in the nature of authentic faith to solve our personal problems. It would be more accurate to say that faith is supposed to help us live with our problems, live with our anguish and heartache, and help us continue to pray for our adult offspring without ever giving up hope, no matter what.

If our faith depends on God bringing an adult son or daughter back to the Church and to the practice of the Catholic faith, that's not faith; it's a way to control others and make them do what we want. This is actually a childish kind of faith, one that is contingent on God doing what we want him to do. But God doesn't work like that. God respects our children's free will, and if they choose a direction in life that leads away from the Church, he allows them to do that. God leaves our adult children free, and we need to do the same, without giving up praying for them, because that is what authentic faith does: it prays for others without insisting on specific results. Real faith leaves free adult offspring who wander from the Church while being always ready to welcome them back if and when they choose to return.

Does it do no good, then, to pray for wandering adult offspring? On the contrary. Prayer bears fruit in the lives of those we pray for, but not always in the specific ways we have in mind. Real faith prays for others but leaves the specifics to the mystery of God's will. Yes, it's a source of real heartache if our adult offspring abandon the faith they were raised in. But faith is not supposed to be a solution to this problem. Rather, faith prays in nonspecific terms—that God's will, for example, may be done for the one we pray for—and leaves the rest to the mystery of God's love for the person(s). We may pray and be left with an apparent nonresponse from God, but faith continues to pray all the same.

Authentic faith reflects and expresses the utter mystery that is our relationship with God, and faith leaves the mystery intact. Faith doesn't snap its fingers at mystery and make it go away. Rather, if anything, authentic faith intensifies the mystery so that, paradoxically, you find yourself aware that life has meaning only in the context of this mystery. You see only through unseeing. You understand because you have faith, whereas faith-as-solution-to-problems believes only to the extent that it can understand, and the natural result is despair.

Authentic faith lives with the constant realization that authentic Christian prayer does not work like magic. As we saw in an earlier chapter, in its technical meaning "magic" means to make something happen by reciting the correct words and/or performing the correct actions with the correct objects. Magic gives a human being absolute control over superhuman forces. But Christian prayer is not magic. Rather, Christian prayer is communion with the God who is Love, and it leaves all things with God's good care regardless of apparent results or lack of results.

The prayer of authentic faith is, ultimately, a prayer of complete trust in God, no matter what, whether problems remain or go away. In a book published in 1941, English Catholic author Caryll Houselander (1901–1954) told a story that illustrates this point:

> Lately I learned something that made me understand as never before the beauty of the habit of prayer. A Jew was telling me that he so wished in these days [during World War II] that he had faith; he was building a sandbag wall and foolishly I had dropped my crucifix into it; he insisted on undoing his wall and getting it for me. He was a stranger, and I did not know him; he was standing holding my crucifix, looking at it with a puzzled wistfulness. "Of course," he said, "I'm a Jew, my mother was a good Jewess, I never learned nothing about Christ, and we don't bother to, but I did learn to say my prayers day and night, and I wish I 'ad kept it up."
>
> "What did you say?" I asked.
>
> "Well, the morning ones was long, but the night was short; all us little Jew kids said it as we fell asleep."
>
> "What was it?"
>
> "Well, Miss, it went like this: 'Father, into Thy hands I commend my spirit.' It's what mothers taught little Jewish boys ever since the world began, they do say. They tells 'em to say it just before they falls asleep."[4]

The prayer Caryll Houselander's Jewish acquaintance learned from his mother is, in fact, the ultimate prayer behind all other prayers—or at least it should be. This is the prayer of authentic faith, the prayer of a faith that does not think of itself as a magic solution to problems or an antidote to anxiety. The prayer of Jesus as he died on the cross expresses the kind of adult faith we're talking about here: "Father, into your hands I commend my spirit."

Much of the time, if faith disappoints us it is because that faith fails to solve a problem for us or fails to get results of a particular kind that we have in mind. Other people do not change, the world does not change, or we do not get our way exactly as we had in mind. But this "faith" is little more than an escapist fantasy and a misunderstanding of what faith truly is. For if faith solves any problems it does so only by helping us see that a problem is simply an opportunity for trust. A problem or source of anxiety is an opportunity to place our trust in God's love both for us and for anyone else who is involved in the situation we have in mind that we wish God would do something about.

This is true of faith not only on a personal level, however. It is also true of faith within the Church, faith as the most basic characteristic of those who by their membership constitute the Church, or *are* the Church. Consider some words of Thomas Merton:

> Since I am a Catholic, I believe, of course, that my Church guarantees for me the highest spiritual freedom. I would not be a Catholic if I did not believe this. I would not be a Catholic if the Church were merely an organization, a collective institution with rules and laws demanding external conformity from its members.
>
> I see the laws of the Church, and all the various ways in which she exercises her teaching authority and her jurisdiction, as subordinate to the Holy Spirit and the law of love. I know that my Church does not look like this to those who are outside her; to them the Church acts on a principle of authority but not of freedom. They are mistaken. It is in Christ and in His Spirit that true freedom is found, and the Church is His Body, living by His Spirit.[5]

This Catholic connection between personal faith and the Church is a scandal to more than a few people, and not just those who are irreligious. It is a scandal to many Protestant Christians and members of non-Christian religions, too, because, as Merton said, they think that the Church is about authority, not freedom. But at its core, the Church, the community of faith, beckons us to live as the First Letter of Peter teaches: "As servants of God, live as free people, yet do not use your freedom as a pretext for evil" (2:16).

A faith that presents itself as a solution to all problems is no faith at all but an illusion, as insubstantial as a morning mist that vanishes the moment it is exposed to the light of the sun. Faith leaves you with your problems and troubles, but because of faith you are no longer a slave to your problems and troubles. Rather, you are a free person who stands on your own two feet to deal with your problems and troubles with the patience and love of the Risen Christ.

Faith is not a way to escape death

Search through the words and pithy sayings of the saints and Doctors of the Church—a title given to certain saints for their outstanding teachings—on the topic of death. Here are a few to give you the general drift of what they have to say:

> The foolish fear death as the greatest of evils, the wise desire it as a rest after their labors and the end of ills.
>
> *Saint Ambrose* (340–397)

~

> Blessed be God for our sister, the death of the body.
>
> *Saint Francis of Assisi* (1181–1226)

~

> For man is by nature afraid of death and of the dissolution of the body; but there is this most startling fact, that he

who has put on the faith of the cross despises even what is
naturally fearful, and for Christ's sake is not afraid of death.

Saint Athanasius (295–373)

~

Life is given us that we may learn to die well, and we never
think of it! To die well we must live well.

Saint John Vianney (1786–1859)

Certainly it is clear from both Scripture and Sacred Tradition that
Christian faith brings a union with Christ that is a real and mystical
sharing in both his death and resurrection. As St. Paul writes in his
Letter to the Romans:

> Do you not know that all of us who have been baptized into
> Christ Jesus were baptized into his death? Therefore we have
> been buried with him by baptism into death, so that, just as
> Christ was raised from the dead by the glory of the Father,
> so we too might walk in newness of life. For if we have been
> united with him in a death like his, we will certainly be
> united with him in a resurrection like his (6:3–5).

In other words, Christian faith means that the death we must
experience is no longer just our death but a mystical and real sharing
in the death of Christ, and because that is so we will also share in his
Resurrection to eternal life—whatever good and glorious mystery
these words may refer to. Through our loving God's gift of himself to
us in the sacrament of baptism, our death becomes a sharing in the
death of Christ, and his Resurrection becomes our destiny, too.

All this we know by faith—that is, by experience of our mystical
and real union with Christ in this life. But this does not mean that
death becomes a mere illusion. By no means. Sometimes people think
of faith as a way to escape death or to render death a mere illusion. On
the contrary, just as the historical Jesus of Nazareth experienced an
actual human death—and in a much more profound way than most
of us will ever experience it, through torture and slow execution—so
we will experience human death with all that this implies. Faith is no
escape from the experience of death. But just as Jesus accepted his

death, even embraced it as God's will for him, so faith invites each person to accept his or her death as the unique event that it is.

What difference, then, does faith make when it comes to death? For the Christian, faith means that your death cannot be separated from Christ's death. For the Christian dies *in Christ*, and we should never underestimate the meaning of this truth. For to die "in Christ" is the exact opposite understanding of death than the view for which death is equal to oblivion. Father Karl Rahner, S.J., arguably the greatest Catholic theologian of the twentieth century, wrote:

> To the innermost reality of the world there belongs what we call Jesus Christ in his life and death, what was poured out over the cosmos at the moment when the vessel of his body was shattered in death, and Christ actually became, even in his humanity, what he had always been by his dignity, the heart of the universe, the innermost center of all created reality.[1]

To die "in Christ" is to find unity with "the heart of the universe, the innermost center of all created reality." Thus, for the Christian, death has a unique *meaning*. But this does not mean that death for the Christian has become unreal or an illusion. Rather, the death of the one who lives by faith looks exactly identical to the death of one who does not live by faith. As far as all the external, observable phenomena associated with death are concerned, dead is dead, no matter if the person lived by faith or not. As far as the physical experience of death is concerned, the person of faith passes through death exactly like anyone else passes through death.

So faith is no escape hatch when it comes to death. The difference that faith makes is entirely real, of course, but it is also entirely personal. In other words, the difference that faith makes is in forming your attitude toward death and the vision with which you approach and even welcome the great mystery of death when it comes.

Karl Rahner wrote many times of the importance of approaching death with a fundamental openness and "with unconditional readiness in faith for the incomprehensible God."[2] What matters in faith is the capacity to be open to death consciously aware of your union with Christ's death "by which Christ inserted his divine life into the world itself."[3]

In other words, the pithy quotations at the beginning of this chapter are *all* true, even though they may seem to include contradictions. It is quite true that authentic faith leads you to not fear death. But it does not mean you escape death. To repeat what St. John Vianney said, "Life is given us that we may learn to die well . . ." Authentic faith leads you to face and accept your own mortality in a culture that is in denial about mortality at every turn. You may think about anything and everything, the dominant culture cries, except death! After all, death is *terrifying*, and you don't want to think about that. Because if you do, you might not want to take so seriously the pursuit of—well, financial security, which is, at least for the dominant culture, the *ultimate* form of security.

This is the truth, as even the dominant culture knows. If you think about your own mortality, about the *fact* that you have a finite, a limited, number of days, hours, and minutes to stand upright, breathe in and out, move about on your own, then you might begin to think that there are some things more important than, yes, even financial security. Authentic faith carries this difference, however. Authentic faith whispers the truth that, far from being morbid to ponder, your own eventual demise can be a source of healing and liberation. If you can imagine that. If you can.

Poet, essayist, and small-town funeral director Thomas Lynch writes thus:

> The facts of life and death remain the same. We live and die, we love and grieve, we breed and disappear. And between these existential gravities, we search for meaning, save our memories, leave a record for those who will remember us.[4]

Here you have it, the way that faith, authentic faith, figures into the big picture. Faith is for filling in the spaces "between these existential gravities." If faith has anything to contribute, it is not to help us find some back door we can use to slip away from death—no. Rather, faith offers that illusive mortar we call *meaning*. Faith helps the living and dying, the loving and grieving, the breeding and disappearing *make sense*, hang together; it helps the pieces to fall into place. Faith, authentic faith, whispers in our hearts that it is good to save our memories and prepare some record for those we leave behind, for those who will follow us in death, but later in time, later.

Faith whispers in our hearts that death is real, rock solid, can be relied upon as surely as little green apples can call their maker God. Faith whispers in our hearts that the only thing more certain than death is that on both this side of death and the other side of death there is a source of security even more reliable than greenbacks—moolah—clams, insurance policies, and money market accounts. Here, and there, is the Ultimately Reliable One who is Love.

Here is the long and the short of it: faith offers no escape from death. Death remains a dark mystery, and everyone must die, even you. But faith does do *something*. Faith says that death is not the ultimate reality. Yes, you must die. Yes, you don't have to like it. But settle into your life, both the dark and the light times, and you will find that you will learn a lesson, and the lesson is this: ultimately, it's all about the light, not the darkness. The darkness does not go away, it keeps turning up. But when you give yourself up in trust on the verge of the darkness called death, well, on the other side of the thin veil between here and there, now and then, you will find not darkness, only light, light, and eternal light.

Faith leads to an ongoing exercise or strategy or attitude as you go along through your life—an exercise or strategy or attitude that actually tries to befriend death, or darkness, in small ways so that when the Big Darkness, death, presents itself, you won't be complete strangers. This exercise or strategy or attitude traditionally is called *asceticism*. Monks and nuns once included ascetical practices in their regular spiritual practices. They fasted with some rigor. They purposely caused themselves physical discomfort, even outright pain, and did not call it masochism, and often it truly was not. You can read the stories of saints who wore barbed wire around the waist, under their clothing, put pieces of gravel in their shoes, and "took the discipline," which meant using a small whip to flog oneself on one's bare back. Stories are told of saints who slept in coffins to remind themselves of death, or meditated upon skulls, not Hamlet-like, philosophically, but to sober themselves about their ultimate end in time and space. All of which strike us enlightened moderns as bizarre, at best, morbid at worst.

Today, of course, the old monks' and nuns' ascetical customs do not make us want to follow their example. But we can learn from those old holies. They knew the capacity of the human heart to kid itself constantly, right down the line, about escaping death. They knew that we are all like the writer William Saroyan who wrote short stories (*The Daring Young Man on the Flying Trapeze* [1934]) and plays (*The Time of Your Life* [1939]). In 1981, dying of cancer, Saroyan phoned the Associated Press and dictated a statement to the effect that when it came to death, he always thought that he would be the exception. "Now what?" he concluded.

We all think that we will be the exception. But one of the most important purposes of the best in the Christian ascetical tradition is to help us anticipate death in healthy, healing, liberating ways. Take fasting, for example. Authentic faith embraces healthy fasting, not because food is bad or the pleasure of eating is bad, but precisely to *deny the self*. Fasting is one response to a teaching of Jesus: "If any want to become my followers, let them deny themselves and take up their cross and follow me" (Mark 8:34).

Self-denial is not denial of the goodness of food or eating, but *self*-denial. A traditional way to put this in different words is "to die to oneself." So the purpose of fasting, as well as other ascetical practices, is to *anticipate death*. When you fast, you deny yourself a simple pleasure, and you deny yourself a bit of the material sustenance needed for life to continue. You take a little taste of death. Not for morbid reasons do you do this, of course, but for the sake of a life that transcends physical life and to cultivate a bit of freedom from the demands of your physical appetites. You fast in order to be free to respond more freely to the invitation of Christ to "follow me."

All three parts of the teaching of Jesus are essential, to "deny" yourself, to "take up" your "cross" and to "follow" Christ. When you fast, your faith anticipates death and accepts mortality, the direct opposite of a faith that thinks of itself as a way to escape death. Authentic faith accepts the need to deny the self because even in life we need to learn how to die well, with a spirit open to greater life.

Of course, the most important asceticism comes in forms we don't choose in advance, not, at least, in the particulars. For example, when you make any major life commitment, the result is both cross and resurrection. When you choose to marry a particular person, you acknowledge in the abstract that every day will not be filled with pure, unadulterated bliss. But the actual ways darkness, difficulties, conflict, and so forth enter into your life together are not ways you would choose for yourself. These difficult moments—and days and weeks— become genuine forms of asceticism, ways to anticipate death for the sake of greater spiritual freedom, when we accept them for the sake of love. Far more valuable than a relatively artificial practice, such as fasting, are the difficult times that come to us uninvited in daily life, and in our relationships with those with whom we live and work. Such experiences constitute asceticism in the best sense of the word.

When you accept the pain, anxiety, and inconvenience children bring into your life, you "practice" for dying one day. When you do not try to avoid the difficulty of working through conflict with your spouse, you anticipate death for the sake of spiritual healing and liberation. When you set aside your own preferences in favor of someone else's preferences, you experience a little bit of death to self, which helps you prepare your heart for the real death that will come at the end of your life.

Of course, none of these ascetical practices make any sense apart from faith. So it is precisely faith that motivates and supports a practice such as fasting or the simple acceptance of the "crosses" that come with everyday life. Authentic faith helps you not to escape death but to accept it in trust and self-abandonment to God's incomprehensible love.

Faith, in other words, does not help us avoid death, but we do expect faith to help us cope with the fact of our own death and that of others, particularly those we love. Authentic Christian faith does this, as we suggested earlier, from the context of the death and resurrection of Jesus. This faith—this ongoing experience of intimacy with the Risen Christ—teaches us that life is transformed through death, not obliterated by death, and that our hope for personal immortality is reasonable. When we think of death as an enemy, St. Francis of Assisi reminds us otherwise by singing of death as a "sister."

At the same time, authentic Christian faith always has a communal character. Even though, ultimately, we live and die alone, our journey through life is in the company of the communion of saints—a community that includes but transcends time and space. Thus, when we die, we do not leave this community behind. Authentic faith establishes us as members of the communion of saints. We both live and die in the company of "so great a cloud of witnesses" (Hebrews 12:1) that even death remains a communal experience.

An adult understanding of faith leads us, however, to an adult understanding of the terms that surround a faith response to death. In other words, when we hear and use phrases such as "resurrection of the body," "judgment," and "heaven," an adult conception of faith reminds us that all such language is metaphorical and symbolic. No human words can adequately express the mysteries that these words attempt to express. Nevertheless, these words point to realities, not illusions.

Authentic faith helps us trust in the realities that the traditional words and phrases refer to without taking the old words and phrases literally. Death is real. Faith does not mean we will avoid death. But faith does mean that death has only the penultimate, not the ultimate, word. There is no avoiding death, but there is Something Else after death, in—for lack of better words—a condition we call "eternity." Whatever that may mean.

In other words, death confronts us with the mystery of What Happens Next, and in a very real sense we haven't the slightest idea. Here is where authentic faith comes into play, however. Faith gives no cognitive knowledge about What Happens Next, but it does give the kind of knowledge the heart can have. Faith makes it possible to trust without having the kind of information science craves or the kind of knowledge that comes from the senses. Faith informs us not through our intellect but through our heart, and the result is the capacity for trust in the face of the mystery of death. On its deathbed, the faith-filled heart finds it possible to say, with Jesus on the cross, "Father, into your hands I commend my spirit" (Luke 23:46).

Now it is also true that authentic faith, when it informs the heart, does not do so in a way contrary to reason. Faith informs the heart, yes, but it does not do so in a way that contradicts anything the intellect can know. Faith completes or fulfills the intellect; it doesn't deny or conflict with the intellect. When faith tells the heart, in the face of death, that it makes perfect sense to trust in self-abandonment to God, the intellect cannot say, "But that's unreasonable." Even the intellect must acknowledge that trust based on personal experience is perfectly reasonable, and that is what the heart would do—trust based on personal experience.

The personal experience the faith-filled heart depends upon in order to trust in God on the brink of death is personal experience of God's loving presence. This is a loving presence that cannot be proven by science, but it is a loving presence the faith-filled heart finds it impossible to deny. Faith finds it just as impossible to deny God as it would be for science to deny the existence of the sun, the moon, and the stars. Indeed, science says, "There are the sun, the moon, and the stars," while faith says, echoing Dante's *Paradiso*, "And here is the Love that moves the sun and the other stars." Faith finds it just as impossible to deny this Love as science finds it impossible to deny the Milky Way.

Science has nothing to say about death except that it *does* happen; it also offers the facts about *how* it happens. People die. Faith, too, acknowledges that death is real. But faith declares that there is Something More, whereas science refuses to say anything unless it has input from the five senses—data it can see, feel, taste, hear, and smell. Faith welcomes all such input but adds that there is a form of knowledge that includes but is not limited to input from the senses. In the words of seventeenth-century mathematician and philosopher Blaise Pascal (1623–1662), "The heart has its reasons which reason does not understand."

Faith declares that the death that happens at the end of life is not entirely unique—or at least, it shouldn't be unique. Because authentic faith is an ongoing mystical and real participation in both the death and resurrection of Christ, faith is no stranger to death. Authentic faith is no stranger to death during life and so faith is no stranger to death at the end of life. Rather than running from death, faith walks with death yesterday, today, and tomorrow. Faith walks with death not as an enemy but as a friend and companion.

Far from being a morbid preoccupation, the companionship between authentic faith and death happens because faith knows that death and resurrection are inseparable. Indeed, not just death but death *and* resurrection are faith's constant companions, both being necessary to the other. Recall once again the words of St. Paul:

> Do you not know that all of us who have been baptized into Christ Jesus were baptized into his death? Therefore we have been buried with him by baptism into death, so that, just as Christ was raised from the dead by the glory of the Father, so we too might walk in newness of life. For if we have been united with him in a death like his, we will certainly be united with him in a resurrection like his (Romans 6:3–5).

Authentic faith places you in a position characterized not by gloom and a bleak outlook on life. Rather, it places you in a stronger position to be hopeful, and it gives you a launching pad, as it were, from which to take risks based on faith. With authentic faith, you find yourself with a capacity to trust—like and with Christ—in the power and providence of a loving Father God whose love is unconditional. This authentic-faith position means that personal suffering, whether physical or emotional, is always penultimate, never the final fact of anyone's existence.

Here is a truth that is both difficult and mysterious, one that only faith can make any sense of: pain and suffering, for authentic Christian faith, are one with an ongoing mystical and real participation in the suffering and death of Christ—with his cross that leads to his Resurrection. In other words, pain and suffering are, for authentic faith, aspects of the ongoing experience of death in this life, an experience that anticipates the death that comes at the end of natural life. Yet this death is anything but isolating or individualistic.

Awareness of an ongoing participation in the suffering and death of Christ leads authentic faith not to withdraw from others, but ever closer to the heart of the community of faith. This means that pain, suffering, and the death they anticipate opens faith to receive the support of others, and it opens faith to those who would share their own feelings of alienation and loss, pain and suffering—in other words, their own experience of death-in-the-midst-of-life. Authentic faith both shares with others its ongoing experience of death and remains open to the pain, suffering, and dying of others.

Faith does not see death and try to run the other direction because faith seeks not unreality but reality. Authentic faith recognizes in death the ultimate opportunity to unite oneself with the real and the true. The way you respond to death reveals your most basic disposition toward God in all of life. Awareness and acceptance of death throughout life enables you to cultivate a humble and obedient acceptance of your finitude and your absolute dependence on God. Death reminds you that in time and space you had a beginning and you will have an end, that you did not bring yourself into existence, and you have no power to keep yourself in existence permanently. To acknowledge this leaves you with a choice for either trust in God or disbelief in one form or another and, ultimately, despair.

Faith chooses to face and accept death, even in the midst of life, and to trust in God in the face of this great and seemingly dark mystery. There are some sayings that survive from the Desert Fathers who lived lives of prayer and asceticism in the deserts of Egypt, Palestine, Arabia, and Persia, in the fourth century. Here is one saying:

> Abbot Joseph asked Abbot Pastor: Tell me how I can become a monk. The elder replied: If you want to have rest here in this life and also in the next, in every conflict with another say: Who am I? And judge no one.[5]

Awareness and humble acceptance of death is not just a private spiritual exercise. Faith encourages this acceptance, and it has a direct impact on all of our relationships with other people. If we humbly acknowledge that we are moving toward our own death, and the same is true for all the other people we know, that helps us be more patient and more compassionate with others. Not only that, but it helps us to be faithful to our most basic commitments.

When, for example, husband and wife, friends, or even employee and manager, truly believe that they and the other are finite creatures carrying the seeds of their own death, that helps them to be patient and persistent with each other. It helps them to be patient with conflict, patient with each other's shortcomings, and more ready to forgive and be reconciled when these are called for.

Authentic faith inspires awareness and acceptance of death, and that helps us to keep our promises. It helps us to not take anything, even life itself, too seriously. Hey, I'm going to die, you're going to die. Life is too short for anything but patience, persistence, quiet thankfulness for blessings large and small. Life is too short for anything but ready forgiveness and a prompt return to life, life, life.

When she learned that she had a terminal form of cancer, Caryll Houselander wrote: "I honestly long to be told 'a hundred percent cure' and to return to this life and celebrate it with gramophone records, giggling, and gin."[6]

This is what faith does. It chooses life even on the doorstep of death. Faith accepts death because it knows that death is the doorway to life beyond imagining.

Faith is not the answer to all questions

One of the most common objections to Christian faith raised by skeptics is that people of faith think they have all the answers to life's biggest questions and deepest mysteries. As with all misconceptions of faith, skeptics have reason to think this, for there are not a few religious people who give the impression that they have the Great Mysteries all sewed up. In many, if not most cases, however, these religious people embrace a simpleminded fundamentalism of some sort. Either that, or they substitute a simpleminded piety for authentic faith—and while genuine piety and genuine faith can and should co-exist, they are definitely not the same.

Typically, biblical fundamentalists are sectarian Protestants who believe in biblical inerrancy. They believe that nothing in the Bible can possibly be wrong, even historically and scientifically. If something appears to be wrong that just means we haven't discovered the truth the Bible refers to yet.[1]

In a parallel path, Catholic fundamentalists believe that, in effect, no matter what the pope says, or what official Vatican documents declare, in both cases it might as well be God speaking. Whether Protestant biblical or Catholic fundamentalism, the underlying concept of faith is one that thinks of faith as a source of absolutely reliable answers to whatever questions may arise. Now, certainly the Bible has plenty of a reliable nature to say about life, faith, and the meaning of it all. But it does not have ready-made answers to all questions and conundrums, and it reflects an understanding of the cosmos and human nature no thinking person today can take literally.

Just try to get the Bible to tell you whether it is right or wrong to practice artificial insemination by donor, or whether wetlands should be protected from development. Certainly, the pope's words are much more likely to embody wisdom than the pronouncements of celebrities and the pressures of the dominant popular culture. But even official Catholic teaching presents the pope as speaking infallibly only under extremely rare circumstances. Perhaps the best concise explanation of infallibility is found in the Glossary of the *Catechism of the Catholic Church*:

> The gift of the Holy Spirit to the Church whereby the pastors of the Church, the pope and the bishops in union with him, can definitively proclaim a doctrine of faith or morals for the belief of the faithful. . . This gift is related to the inability of the whole body of the faithful to err in matters of faith and morals.[2]

Any understanding of faith that attributes to that faith a way to answer all questions misses the point entirely when it comes to understanding authentic faith. Faith is not, and never can be, a sort of always-active answer machine. If anything, faith leaves you with more unanswered questions than you had before, for authentic faith brings you into an "up-close" situation with Absolute Mystery.

Intellectually, at least, faith brings a kind of darkness because it is so bright. Thomas Merton explained it this way:

> The very obscurity of faith is an argument of its perfection. It is darkness to our minds because it so far transcends their weakness. The more perfect faith is, the darker it becomes. The closer we get to God, the less is our faith diluted with the half-light of created images and concepts. Our certain-

ty increases with this obscurity, yet not without anguish and even material doubt, because we do not find it easy to subsist in a void in which our natural powers have nothing of their own to rely on. And it is in the deepest darkness that we most fully possess God on earth, because it is then that our minds are most truly liberated from the weak, created lights that are darkness in comparison to Him; it is then that we are filled with His infinite Light which seems pure darkness to our reason.[3]

Of course, Merton's drift was shaped by his own interests as a contemplative monk. But what he says applies equally to any assumption that faith should provide you with a ready made set of answers to all kinds of profound, brow-furrowing questions.

Yes, faith gives some answers. Authentic faith puts you in a place where you "know" that life has meaning, that it is not absurd. But its "answers" are not the kinds of answers you get from a scientific worldview. Indeed, the "answers" you get from faith tend to be both adequate and inadequate, satisfying and unsatisfying. This is so because these "answers" come from the encounter of a finite being—you—with the Infinite God, and there is only so much your little noggin can hold. The "answers" faith gives tend to be more satisfying to the heart than to the mind. Of course, as Catholicism's traditional affection for the intellectual life shows, authentic faith can never deny or contradict reason; instead, genuine faith completes or fulfills reason.

Human beings ask, "Why am I here? Where did I come from? What is my ultimate destiny?" The experience of faith provides the "answer" of an ongoing relationship with God, whose love is unconditional. Reflection on the historic faith community's experience of this relationship resulted in the Scriptures and lesser writings, each with its own kind of authority. A good example of the latter in our own era is the *Catechism of the Catholic Church*. In such documents, we find "answers" of a more formulaic nature, "answers" that attempt to interpret the wisdom the faith community has learned from its relationship with God in the course of many centuries.

This is how we end up with answers such as, "God created everything that exists" and "The purpose of life is to love God and neighbor" and "Death is a transition from temporal life to eternal life." This is how we get beautiful, true, but only partially satisfying words such as the opening paragraph in the *Catechism of the Catholic Church*:

> God, infinitely perfect and blessed in himself, in a plan of sheer goodness freely created man to make him share in his own blessed life. For this reason, at every time and in every place, God draws close to man. He calls man to seek him, to know him, to love him with all his strength. He calls together all men, scattered and divided by sin, into the unity of his family, the Church. To accomplish this, when the fullness of time had come, God sent his Son as Redeemer and Savior. In his Son and through him, he invites men to become, in the Holy Spirit, his adopted children and thus heirs of his blessed life.[4]

Believers and outside observers alike may get the impression from the sheer volume of church documents and formal teachings that faith is *supposed* to give you answers of all kinds in great abundance. But not so. Church documents and formal teachings are true as far as they go, to be sure, and they serve a valid purpose. But as "answers" they often raise as many questions as they respond to.

For example, many English-speaking people today find that the noninclusive character of this translation of the *Catechism* from the Latin text raises questions all by itself. The term "men," for example, no longer encompasses all people, male and female, as it once did. Although an even more thorny issue, and one not so easily resolved as references to human beings, is the objection to using masculine pronouns (*he, him*) to refer to God who, obviously, has neither masculine nor feminine gender but who, metaphorically, at least, must be said to include both. But in English at least, how else do we have to represent God as personal except by using masculine and/or feminine pronouns? To resort to functional titles such as "Creator God" or "Birthing God" seems a feeble effort, at best. So right there you have an official church document that, by its nature as a translation, in the very act of articulating answers raises questions almost impossible to resolve.

Even if we disregard these not insignificant questions, however, and pay attention to one of the answers the text makes, we still find ourselves left with questions. The catechism says that "at every time and in every place, God draws close to man." But if this is so, what about times and places of profound evil? Among the most obvious places and times we can ask about are the Nazi death camps during World War II. Did God draw close to the people in places as unspeakably evil as Dachau and Auschwitz? For that matter, does God draw close in any time and situation where the rights and dignity of human beings are trampled upon or disregarded by other human beings? How can we say that God draws close when an innocent child suffers? Is God present at a meeting of a racist hate group?

The catechism continues, saying that God "calls together all men, scattered and divided by sin, into the unity of his family, the Church." This "answer" can only leave the intelligent reader with questions such as, "Does this mean *everyone*? Is the catechism saying that even non-Christians are called into the Catholic Church? Aren't Jews, Muslims, and Buddhists likely to find this offensive?"

In other words, even—or perhaps especially—the "answers" that come from official teachings of the faith community tend to be less than completely satisfying to the questioning mind. So even in this sense faith cannot be said to offer cut-and-dried answers to important questions. Official church documents, such as the *Catechism of the Catholic Church* and the documents issued by the Second Vatican Council in the mid-1960s are good—again, as far as they go—but no one can say that they offer final, definitive, completely adequate answers to even the most basic human questions. Rather, they are feeble human attempts to shed some light in the darkness, much better than nothing but hardly the firm and final last word on anything. We can, and should, cull much wisdom from such documents, but we need to keep in mind that revisions are always possible, even probable.

Far more satisfying, yet still marked by human historical and cultural limitations we need to take seriously, are the Scriptures—the so-called "Old" and "New" Testaments that make up the Bible. Unlike documents such as the *Catechism of the Catholic Church*, papal encyclicals, and the like, the Hebrew and Christian Scriptures are said to be "inspired," that is, authored in some ultimate sense by God. A theological dictionary defines inspiration thus:

> The special impulse and guidance of the Holy Spirit through which the books of scripture were composed and

so can be called the word of God . . . What God had to say
is found in what was said by the human writers, who were
genuine authors and not mere stenographers copying down
what God dictated. . . .[5]

Scripture is superior in value to official church documents in the
sense that those who author official church documents must use
Scripture as the ultimate standard against which to measure what they
write. Of course, official church documents participate in and are a
part of Sacred Tradition—but only to the extent that they accurately
express the entire Church's experience of faith in particular historical
and cultural circumstances.

The Scriptures are rooted in the unrepeatable foundational experiences of both Judaism and Christianity, which also gives them a
unique value. Too, the Scriptures cannot be said to offer "answers"
except in the context of faith experience. In other words, the "answers"
the Scriptures give are far more satisfying for those who read them in
the faith context in which they were written, rather than "from the
outside," as it were, from some theoretical pure objectivity. The
Scriptures speak from faith to faith, that is, *from* the experience of intimacy with God to the experience of intimacy with God.

The same is true of official church documents, of course, but
rather than trying to speak from and to contemporary human experience, as official church documents do, the Scriptures speak from and
to an experience that both includes and transcends history. This
means that the Scriptures have a timeless quality even while they
remain couched in the historical periods in which they were written.
The "answers" found in the Bible, then, are not so much answers as
they are road signs pointing in the right direction.

Much of the value of the Scriptures comes from the fact that the
various human authors of the biblical documents used particular literary styles. The "answers" the Bible gives come in literary forms from
poetry to fiction and from letters to fantasy. All these literary forms
communicate truth, but to say that they answer questions in a scientific or historical fashion would be to miss the point entirely. Even in
the Scriptures we can't say that faith provides a ready-made set of
answers.

In fact, the "answers" to life's Big Issues that we find in the Bible
can hardly be called answers at all. It is true that, for example, the

Hebrew Scriptures, or Old Testament, give us the so-called Ten Commandments.[6] But it doesn't take someone with an advanced degree in Scripture studies to tell you that the Ten Commandments— a more accurate translation of the Hebrew renders "commandments" as "words" or "utterances"—are far from being crystal clear, specific "answers."[7]

Like Scripture in general, the Ten Commandments are not so much answers as they orient us in the right direction, and when it comes to specific questions and issues, they say, "Using your faith and your heart and the brain God gave you, figure it out for yourself." The same is true when it comes to the teachings of Jesus in the Gospels. We can say that Jesus responds to the question, "What is the meaning and purpose of life?" In the Gospel of Mark, for example, when a scribe asks Jesus which commandment is the greatest of all, he responds:

> "The first is, 'Hear, O Israel: the Lord our God, the Lord is one; you shall love the Lord your God with all your heart, and with all your soul, and with all your mind, and with all your strength.' The second is this, 'You shall love your neighbor as yourself.' There is no other commandment greater than these" (12:29–31).

We can take this as Jesus' teaching on the meaning and purpose of life, to be sure. But his words hardly constitute an "answer." They are more like the giving of an orientation in life. We are still left with the question about what we should do, specifically, with our unique, particular life. There are no "answers" about this forthcoming from the New Testament, no matter how diligently we search.

Is it not true, however, that faith means that you agree with and accept certain truths revealed by God? So does this not mean that faith provides at least *some* answers in the form of these revealed truths? Yes. And no. Again, none of the truths revealed by faith are specific answers to specific questions. Rather, they are truths that place life in general, and each individual life in particular, in a certain meaningful context and give a certain general orientation. Within this context and this orientation, each person must still—to use the words of St. Paul—"work out your own salvation with fear and trembling" (Philippians 2:12).

The truths revealed by God that faith makes it possible to accept are expressed in human words and concepts that rely entirely on metaphors, analogies, and philosophical/theological abstractions. As the *Catechism of the Catholic Church* explains:

> Since our knowledge of God is limited, our language about him is equally so. We can name God only by taking creatures as our starting point, and in accordance with our limited human ways of knowing and thinking . . . .
>
> God transcends all creatures. We must therefore continually purify our language of everything that is limited, image-bound or imperfect, if we are not to confuse our image of God—"the inexpressible, the incomprehensible, the invisible, the ungraspable"—with our human representations. Our human words always fall short of the mystery of God.[8]

This means that the "answers" that faith gives are anything but crystal clear answers to questions or solutions to problems. The "truths" of faith come in the form, for example, of formulations such as the Apostles' Creed–the most ancient non-scriptural expression of the "content" of faith that we have, dating back to at least the early 400s, and probably earlier.[9]

Take a close look at the words of this ancient statement of faith:

> I believe in God, the Father almighty,
> Creator of heaven and earth.
> And in Jesus Christ, his only Son, our Lord;
> who was conceived by the Holy Spirit,
> born of the Virgin Mary,
> suffered under Pontius Pilate,
> was crucified, died, and was buried.
> He descended into hell;
> the third day he rose again from the dead;
> he ascended into heaven,
> sits at the right hand of God, the Father almighty;
> from thence he shall come
> to judge the living and the dead.
> I believe in the Holy Spirit,

the holy Catholic Church,
the communion of saints,
the forgiveness of sins,
the resurrection of the body,
and life everlasting. Amen.[10]

Clearly, the Apostles' Creed consists entirely of religious language that speaks the truth *from* faith *to* faith. The "information" that the Apostles' Creed offers is about historical events. But in order to be taken as "answers" about anything, this "information" presupposes faith. The Apostles' Creed is more of a summary narrative about the central events in Christian salvation history than "answers" to basic life questions. To recite the Apostles' Creed with faith and with firm belief in its truths still does not clear up for anyone all questions about the meaning and purpose of life. Rather, it provides a larger context of meaning within which to construct a life that has both meaning and purpose.

The Apostles' Creed is what we might call a resource of religion. It shows that the function of religion is to support, nourish, and express faith. This is what the Apostles' Creed does. But it does not turn faith into a source of answers to the Big Questions. The Apostles' Creed says, "This is what I/we believe." It does not claim to be a set of answers to anything. We recite the Apostles' Creed, and we declare that this is what we, as Christians, believe. But this does not leave us with no questions, no problems, and a clarity of vision and insight to make us the envy of all the world. It leaves us with a basic orientation in life, but it also leaves us with just as many questions as we had before. The difference now is—and granted, this is no small difference—that we search for answers with a trust in the ultimate meaningfulness of the quest itself. We know that even if we do not find all the Answers, ultimately we will find ourselves held securely, healed, and loved by God who is at once both the ultimate Question and the ultimate Answer.

Of course, underlying the idea that faith provides answers to all questions is the false assumption that faith should provide answers to all questions. Certainly, faith does give some answers, but not so much ready-made answers to specific questions. Rather, faith is a source of knowledge and understanding only in the way, analogically, that the relationship between two people who love each other is a source of knowledge and understanding. Because two people are close friends, or because a man and woman commit themselves to a loving marriage, they "know" each other and they "understand" each other. Because they are friends, or because they are married, their love for each other gives them a knowledge and an understanding that make acceptance of each other's mystery possible.

You don't insist that your friend or your spouse act in a "reasonable" manner all the time, or in a way that is "acceptable" to you in each and every instance. Rather, you accept and remain committed to your friend or your spouse even when you don't entirely understand him or her. By way of analogy, this is how faith works, too. Because you have a personal, loving relationship with the Personal Mystery (God) whom you "know" and experience as both your source and your goal, your beginning and your end, you keep on trying to be faithful to this relationship. Even when you fail in this relationship, and even when this Mysterious Love (God) seems to not meet your expectations, still you remain; you continue to be friends, as it were, because you know and trust that somehow God's "behavior" will make sense in the long run. We are, after all, talking about a "Friend" who is far more of a mystery than a human friend could ever be. So with God, you hang in there, trusting that even when a human friend fails you this Mysterious Love will not.

You might say that the "answers" that come from faith are far more valuable than the answers that come from mere sensory input or intellectual processes. All scientific knowledge is subject to revision, after all. A single new discovery, or a single new invention, or a single new insight can change virtually everything. Think of the profound changes brought about in society and culture by the invention of the automobile, for example. Or of the social and cultural transformations caused by the invention of the personal computer or the widespread availability of artificial forms of contraception. For good or for ill, these things arrived due to developments in scientific knowledge, and the world will never be the same. The knowledge that comes from faith, however, is a knowledge that is far deeper than any knowledge that the human brain can ever wrap itself around completely. This does not mean, however, that this knowledge cannot be trusted.

Again, the best analogy is that of human friendship or a loving marriage. No couple would ever marry if they had to first have complete comprehension of each other. Instead, the couple know and understand and trust each other without having a completely reliable scientific basis for their commitment to each other. The commitment we make to God is something like this. We have a relationship with God that transcends, but does not contradict, reason. So what we "know" as a result of our faith is both reasonable and deeper than reason can explain. Just as the love of husband and wife is both reasonable and deeper than reason can explain, so faith gives a similar kind of knowledge about the meaning and purpose of life.

Another way to look at the kinds of knowledge that faith gives is to take seriously our human finitude. We can know and understand only so much, but all that we can learn and understand is consistent with trust in God's love.

Faith is not the opposite of doubt

People sometimes carry around the idea that faith and doubt are incompatible, and perfect faith includes the complete absence of doubts about anything having to do with God, religion, faith, etc. The first thing we need to recall from an earlier chapter is that to ask questions about faith or religious topics does not equal doubt. To ask questions simply means that you want to understand your religion or your faith better. One of the best-known stories in the New Testament illustrates this point. The Gospel of Luke portrays Mary, the future mother of Jesus, as having her questions:

> In the sixth month the angel Gabriel was sent by God to a town in Galilee called Nazareth, to a virgin engaged to a man whose name was Joseph, of the house of David. The virgin's name was Mary. And he came to her and said, "Greetings, favored one! The Lord is with you."
> But she was much perplexed by his words and pondered what sort of greeting this might be. The angel said to her, "Do not be afraid, Mary, for you have found favor with God. And now, you will conceive in your womb and bear a son, and you will name him Jesus. He will be great, and

will be called the Son of the Most High, and the Lord God
will give to him the throne of his ancestor David. He will
reign over the house of Jacob forever, and of his kingdom
there will be no end."

Mary said to the angel, "How can this be, since I am a
virgin?"

The angel said to her, "The Holy Spirit will come upon
you, and the power of the Most High will overshadow you;
therefore the child to be born will be holy; he will be called
Son of God. And now, your relative Elizabeth in her old
age has also conceived a son; and this is the sixth month for
her who was said to be barren. For nothing will be impossible with God."

Then Mary said, "Here am I, the servant of the Lord;
let it be with me according to your word." Then the angel
departed from her (1:26–38).

Mary wants to understand what's up, so she has her questions, and
the Gospel of Luke makes a point of including those questions in its
Annunciation narrative. It's as if Luke wants to tell us that faith not only
allows for questions, but faith without questions isn't much of a faith.

Questions do not equal doubt. There is a sense in which doubt
and faith are incompatible, of course. A theological dictionary, for
example, defines *doubt* thus:

> Uncertainty about or suspension of assent to particular
> Christian beliefs or even to the faith as a whole. Serious
> questions and the honest facing of difficulties do not
> amount to sinful doubt.[1]

If this definition leaves you wondering about the difference
between "doubts" and "serious questions and the honest facing of difficulties," you're not alone. Saint Thomas Aquinas helps us by offer-
ing the following insight:

> Believing . . . means putting faith in something, and this
> resembles knowing in giving firm assent, but resembles
> doubting, suspecting and holding opinions in having no fin-
> ished vision of the truth. So we characterize it as assenting to

> something one is still thinking about. . . . Faith's assent is
> an act of mind not determined by reason but by will.[2]

In other words, you could say that faith, when we take a close look at it, includes the characteristics of both knowing and doubting, for faith never has a "finished vision of the truth." Also—and here Aquinas's words become subtle, indeed—faith is "an act of mind not determined by reason but by will." Does this mean that ultimately faith is unreasonable? By no means.

If we return to our analogy of a trusting relationship between two people—friends or spouses, say—we may better understand Aquinas's point. Ultimately, you trust your friend not because you can tick off the reasons for doing so, but because your friend is your friend. You trust because the one you trust has proven, over the course of your friendship, to be worthy of your trust. Just so, over the course of your relationship with Christ, he has proven worthy of your trust. While you ask your questions and seek better understanding of your faith, you continue to trust precisely because it is reasonable to do so.

When do serious questions become doubts? The difference is one of *meaning*. As long as a question is about meaning it is not a doubt but the expression of a desire to better understand. If you ask, "How can we say that God is love when there is so much suffering in the world?" you are asking a question about meaning. If, on the other hand, you ask, "How can I believe that God is love when there is so much suffering in the world?" you are getting closer to serious doubt. The first question is faith seeking better understanding. The second question comes not from faith but from doubt. As the theological dictionary definition says, however, in order for doubt to be a threat to faith, it must be about "particular Christian beliefs" or "the faith as a whole."

The key issue now becomes a question of *which* Christian beliefs are important enough so that if you genuinely doubt them, they nullify or put at risk your faith itself. The fact is that there are almost endless elements or aspects of the Christian religion that we can doubt up a storm about with no risk to faith whatsoever. To repeat one of my favorite quotations, from G. K. Chesterton: "Catholics know the two or three transcendental truths on which they do agree, and take rather a pleasure in disagreeing on all the rest."

What are these "two or three transcendental truths"? Actually, there are more like seven or eight of them. Recite for yourself the

Apostles' Creed or the Nicene Creed—the one used at Sunday Masses—and you'll get a good summary of the "transcendental truths" that you can question almost endlessly but which won't stand up to much genuine doubt.

This, of course, brings us back to the difference between a question and a doubt. Let's take the first item in the Nicene Creed as we recite it for all Masses on Sundays and Solemnities such as Christmas and Easter: "We believe in one God, the Father, the almighty, maker of heaven and earth, of all that is seen and unseen."

This is the big issue of theological inquiry. Are you or are you not a believer in God? This is an issue that can, and does, bear almost endless questions. Such as: What, exactly, do you mean by the word *God*? Is God all-powerful, and if so why does God allow innocent children to suffer? Is God "personal" or is God a distant and impersonal "Force," uninterested in human affairs? In a more poetic vein, to quote the twentieth-century English poet Stevie Smith, "What care I if good God be / If God be not good to me?" And so on and so forth, *ad infinitum*.

The basic, ground-zero issue, however, is whether or not you acknowledge God's reality. If you are still wondering about this, then you doubt—which is fine, but you are not a person of faith or a religious person. Rather, you are a seeker or someone still trying to settle this issue for yourself. Is God real, or is God just a figment of the human imagination? There are plenty of honest, intellectually responsible people who spend years struggling with this question, living in a state of uncertainty. Which, again, is fine. But it means that such people cannot be said to have faith—not fully, at least. Quite often, when such people do come to faith, they make exceptional believers because they spent time being uncertain.

Sometimes people who lived as believers for many years find themselves wondering about even such basic questions as the reality of God. Intellectually, they begin to question whether there is a God. On the level of the will, however, they do not stop believing. So they cannot be said to be truly in doubt. They continue to choose to believe, but they want to know more, they want to understand God better. Again, this is simply a matter of asking good questions that will lead to a deeper, stronger, more adult faith.

Here we can learn from the great mystics of the Christian tradition. Among the best known is St. John of the Cross, the sixteenth-century Spanish Carmelite who wrote, among other books, *The Dark Night of the Soul*. In the same vein is the late fourteenth-century anonymous author of *The Cloud of Unknowing*, most likely a Carthusian monk and priest. What the author says about the beginnings of contemplative prayer—and what St. John of the Cross says about periods of darkness and aridity in prayer—apply equally to the life of faith in general. *The Cloud of Unknowing* says, "it is usual to feel nothing but a kind of darkness about your mind, or as it were a cloud of unknowing."³

Sometimes, normal dark times in the life of faith can seem like times of genuine doubt, as if faith is gone, replaced by nothing, nothing, nothing at all. This is when it is important to remember that faith is ultimately a matter of the will, not the intellect or imagination. There are times when we do not *feel* love, even for a spouse or children, but this does not mean that we do not love these people. We continue to love on the level where love matters the most, and that is the level of the will. We continue to act on behalf of those we love, even when we don't *feel* love for them.

In a similar manner, you continue to love God, even when you don't *feel* love for God, or even feel his presence in your life. You continue to have faith; you don't stop acting out of faith because, for the time being, you don't *feel* faith. You act in a faithful manner because you *know* in your deepest self that God is real and that even when you don't feel his presence, God remains your Father whose love is absolutely dependable. You continue to say, in your heart, the first words of the Nicene Creed: "I believe in God, the Father, the almighty . . ."

Dark times in the life of faith are not necessarily times of genuine doubt. Rather, they are a normal part of being the human partner in the divine/human relationship called faith. Such times can—even should—lead us to ask questions about faith and about our religion. But we should not mistake various experiences of "the dark night of the soul" as a threat to our faith. Rather, such dark times are an opportunity to become more "grown up" in our faith, to learn that we cannot depend on warm, comforting, emotional feelings in the life of faith. Mystics of all times and places tell us that such feelings are ephemeral and unimportant, the cotton candy of the life of faith, and about as substantial, too.

Ideally, our religion and all its institutional expressions are supposed to be at the service of our faith and of our spirituality. The

Church, as a human institution, is not supposed to be an end in itself. But there are times when our religion and our church fail and fail miserably. There are times when church and religion not only are not helpful but actually act in ways that are harmful or destructive. At such times, we may be inclined to doubt our faith, but such doubts are misplaced. Our Church and our religion are not the object of our faith except in a secondary sense. If we place our faith in church and religion, rather than in God, failures on the part of church and religion are likely to have a destructive effect on our faith—and well they should.

When we say that we "believe in" the Church, we declare that for us, the Church is the place where we believe, the community where our faith is rooted and nurtured, challenged and celebrated. We believe *in* the Church more than we *believe in* the Church. When we understand this, it makes it much easier to tolerate the imperfections and foibles of the Church-as-human-institution. We are less likely, when individuals or groups in the Church cause us pain, to give up on the Church. We are less likely to expect perfection from the Church according to our particular standards of perfection.

Faith and doubt are not strange bedfellows. Rather, they are two sides of the same coin. Doubt and faith are like light and darkness; you can't have one without the other. No matter how strong your faith, doubt will always be tugging at your elbow—because your limited, finite grasp of the Infinite will always be limited and finite. Just as a gallon jug can never contain the whole ocean, so your human intellect and imagination can never fully grasp the Infinite Love revealed by Jesus as your loving Father. Therefore, there will always be the nagging inclination to doubt, and the more you rely exclusively on your intellect the greater will be the temptation to doubt. The more you rely on your whole self, however—intellect, imagination, heart and soul—the less you will be attracted by the darkness of genuine doubt.

Thomas Merton wrote that faith is "not an opinion" and "not a conviction based on rational analysis." It is "not the fruit of scientific evidence."

> Faith is first of all an intellectual assent. It perfects the mind, it does not destroy it. It puts the intellect in possession of Truth which reason cannot grasp by itself. It gives

us certitude concerning God as He is in Himself; faith is
the way to a vital contact with a God Who is alive, and not
to the view of an abstract First Principle worked out by syl-
logisms from the evidence of created things.[4]

In other words, Merton reminds us that faith brings reason into
union with God, which brings about the fulfillment of reason, not its
cancellation. "Blind faith" stifles reason, while authentic faith completes reason. And again, the certainty that faith gives you is not the
certainty that comes from scientific investigation; rather, it's like the
certainty you get from friendship with another person. Your *experience*
of the other person leads you to certainty, for example, about his or
her trustworthiness, even though you could never prove scientifically
to anyone that your certainty about your friend's trustworthiness is
justified. Just so, your *experience* of faith gives you a certitude that God
is worthy of your faith.

This, in turn, means that any doubts you have are relatively unimportant. You go on trusting, you go on having faith, even as you continue asking questions about God, about Christ, and about the
Church, so that you may grow in understanding. Serious doubts about
your faith in itself simply don't enter into the picture because you *know*
the One in whom you trust. Even in the dark times, when God seems
to be a million miles away, you know that he is closer to you than you
are to yourself and is always, always, worthy of complete trust.

Of course, the analogy with friendship has its limits. God, after
all, is not one whom we can see, hear, and touch, as we can a human
friend. Consequently, it can be easy to doubt God's reality on this
basis alone, especially in an age that places such great value on the evidence of the senses. Faith depends on actual human experience of
God, but such experience can seem impossible in a secular culture and
in a world that witnesses gargantuan evils. Doubt can seem the only
reasonable stance in such a world, even doubt to the point of atheism.
Indeed, sometimes it seems that humanistic atheists live more honestly and compassionately than many so-called people of faith.

At the heart of this situation, however, is the need to reject false or
inadequate images or understandings of God. Not infrequently, a person's "atheism" is little more than his or her rejection of inadequate
images of God. Authentic faith wants nothing to do with simpleminded conceptions of God. Indeed, it is not unusual for an "atheism" that

rejects inadequate images of God but lives with compassion to be closer to the truth than a "faith" that has little sensitivity to the needs of others and little sensitivity to God's presence in ordinary, everyday life.

The truth is that even sincere believers may find themselves in moments of doubt and even unbelief. The overwhelming evils of the twentieth century, so recently ended, cannot fail to touch the heart and intellect of people of faith. What matters, however, is that such moments as these do not get a permanent grip on the heart. We do not believe, in other words, that meaninglessness is the final word about anything. Rather, very often to face the darkness of social evils and senseless human cruelty, and not deny their reality, frequently leads the believer to an even deeper faith.

> This faith often is "naked;" what we feel is not faith but anger and fear, doubt, and bitterness. Yet at times of crisis, what crumbles to pieces in us can be a false or immature system of belief rather than faith itself. As we pass through the "dark nights" that life offers us, what had become in us perhaps self-confidence and self-reliance, or a belief system smug, harsh, and intolerant, can be refashioned into a mature faith that clings not to a system or even to feelings of faith but only to God.[5]

In other words, darkness and evil can be an occasion for purifying our faith, for leading us to a faith that is less childish and more mature. A faith that cannot face and work through doubt is a faith that clings to an image of God, and an understanding of faith, that are inadequate.

To repeat, faith and doubt go together, are two sides of the same coin. The experience of true doubt is never an easy experience. But it is an opportunity to leave behind an immature faith and grow in a faith suitable for an adult. You might even say that doubt can be an occasion of grace, a gift from God that invites you to draw closer to the One who is the Father of Jesus and your Father, too.

Afterword

So what *is* faith?

Now that we have explored what faith is *not*, it is only natural to ask what faith *is*. In a sense, it is easier to talk about what faith is not than to explain what faith is, because—as should be clear by now—faith is a great mystery, perhaps *the* great mystery. What faith *is* could easily be the subject of another complete book. For Christian faith is the mystery of the human encounter with God in the Risen Christ.

In fact, we need to make a distinction before we go any farther. Here it is: faith has both an objective and a subjective meaning. Objectively, *faith* refers to "the revealed truth believed in."[1] This is what we mean when we talk about "the faith." The reference is to the entire Christian—more specifically the Catholic—tradition as the source and "depository" of the truth revealed to us in Christ. Once again, you could recite either the Apostles' Creed or the Nicene Creed for a summary of this truth.

The subjective meaning of *faith* is what most of this book is about. The reference here is to the "subjective, personal commitment to God" that is "made possible through the help of the Holy Spirit," and is "a free, reasonable, and total response . . . through which we confess the truth about the divine self-disclosure definitively made in

Christ (John 20:31; Romans 10:9), and entrust our future to God (Romans 6:8; Heb 11:1)."[2]

That is the technical answer to the question, What is faith? Given the tone of this book, however, it is only fair that we try to give a more personal and evocative response to this question.

Faith, Christian faith from a Catholic perspective, is first of all the relationship or personal intimacy that exists between the Risen Christ and the community of those who try to respond to this call to live according to the good news of God's unconditional love for all people and all of creation. Because of a person's membership in this community of faith, for each one faith is an ongoing loving relationship with Christ, and analogically it has the same characteristics as any loving human relationship. It has its ups and downs, and sometimes it can seem beyond understanding, while at other times it can seem as obvious and clear as can be.

Faith gives the kind of "knowledge" close friends or husband and wife have of each other. Faith also gives knowledge of a more cognitive kind, the kind of knowledge about the meaning of life found in the Scriptures, for example, as well as the kinds of knowledge given by Sacred Tradition.

When you try to live as a person of faith—one who does, in fact, have a personal loving relationship with the Risen Lord and with his people, the Church—you want to spend time with him, and you want to spend time in the context of a faith community. So this means you become a person of prayer, someone for whom prayer, in one form or another, is a daily reality. It also means that you feel that you belong to the community of faith the world over, and you feel naturally attracted to be with that community where the Spirit of Christ is present most fully. You become a person who wants to participate regularly when the community of faith gathers to celebrate the Eucharist.

Faith also has a compelling nature. Your faith—your relationship with Christ—pushes you, nudges you all the time, to be more and better, to be more forgiving, more patient, more compassionate, more courageous. Your faith prods you to be more loving, hopeful, and joyful than you would be otherwise.

When it comes to talking about faith, the inclination is either to talk too much or clam up and not talk at all. The experience of faith can be so deep that either is an option. Whether we talk too much about faith, or don't talk about it at all, either can be the wrong choice.

Perhaps we should try to strike the happy medium? Perhaps. We may ask what we can learn from the Tradition about this. Saint Francis of Assisi once said something to the effect that our faith should be so important to us that sometimes we might even want to talk about it. His point was that the most important thing is to *live* our faith; talking about it is of secondary importance.

This is an important point in a society where, in certain circles anyway, there is more than enough talk *about* faith. We need more people who *live* their faith, as there are more than enough who are willing to talk *about* faith, and sometimes talk can be cheap. Yes, there are times when we need to be able to verbalize our faith. But most of the time the best witness to authentic faith is a life lived *in* faith.

We could go on forever. Essentially, however, faith is an unprovable mystery. Faith is not to be taken for granted. One thing you can count on, however: faith is a gift that God will give for the asking. In fact, to ask for faith is to already have faith. The instant you ask, the gift of authentic faith is yours.

Of course, once you have the gift of faith you need to nourish and cultivate it like any delicate seedling. God gives you the gift of faith, and it looks like a tiny seed, but with the sunshine and rain of prayer and participation in the life of the Church and the sacraments, the gift of faith will put down roots and grow to be like the sturdiest of trees in the forest. That much you can count on.

In the end, however, perhaps we are better off with some words from one of the Desert Fathers, Christian hermits who lived in the deserts of Egypt and Syria during the fourth and fifth centuries: "Abbot Sisoes said: Seek God, and not where God lives."[3]

This is the bottom line for authentic faith; it always seeks God in and of himself and for himself. Authentic faith recognizes "where God lives"—including words about God, rituals, and religious institutions—as necessary and valuable. But authentic faith is always on guard against substituting any of the places where God lives for God.

Endnotes

Introduction

1. *Catechism of the Catholic Church*, Second Edition. Washington, D.C.: United States Catholic Conference, Inc., Libreria Editrice Vaticana, 1997, n. 40.
2. Gerald O'Collins, S.J., and Edward G. Farrugia, S.J. *A Concise Dictionary of Theology*, Revised and Expanded Edition (Mahwah, NJ: Paulist Press, 2000), 233.
3. Thomas Merton. *Dancing in the Water of Life: Seeking Peace in the Hermitage*, ed. by Robert E. Daggy (San Francisco: HarperSanFrancisco, 1997), 317.

Chapter One

1. William Shakespeare. *Hamlet*: Act iii, sc. I, 1.
2. For an excellent, more complete discussion of suffering from a scriptural perspective, see Daniel Harrington, S.J., *Why Do We Suffer?* (Franklin, WI: Sheed & Ward, 2000).
3. Gerald O'Collins, S.J., and Edward G. Farrugia, S.J. *A Concise Dictionary of Theology*, Revised and Expanded Edition (Mahwah, NJ: Paulist Press, 2000), 169.
4. *Story of a Soul: The Autobiography of St. Thérése of Lisieux*, trans. by John Clarke, O.C.D. (Washington, D.C.: ICS Publications, 1976).
5. Quoted in Monica Furlong, *Thérése of Lisieux* (New York: Pantheon Books, 1987), 120.
6. Heard by the author in a talk given by John Shea.
7. Joan Meyer Anzia, M.D., and Mary G. Durkin, D. Mn. *Marital Intimacy: A Catholic Perspective* (Chicago: Loyola Press, 1980).
8. Anzia and Durkin. *Ibid.*, 56.
9. Flannery O'Connor. *The Habit of Being*, selected and edited by Sally Fitzgerald (New York: Farrar, Straus & Giroux, 1979), 354.

Chapter Two

1. See Robert A. Krieg, "Gnosticism," in Richard P. McBrien, general editor, *The HarperCollins Encyclopedia of Catholicism* (San Francisco: HarperSanFrancisco, 1995), 563. See also "Gnosticism" in Gerald O'Collins, S.J., and Edward G. Farrugia, S.J., *A Concise Dictionary of Theology*, Revised and Expanded Edition (Mahwah, NJ: Paulist Press, 2000), 96.
2. See Andrew M. Greeley, *Religion as Poetry* (New Brunswick, NJ: Transaction Publishers, 1995).
3. Gerald O'Collins, S.J.. and Edward G. Farrugia, S.J. *A Concise Dictionary of Theology*, Revised and Expanded Edition (Mahwah, NJ: Paulist Press, 2000), 80.

Chapter Three

1. Excerpted from *American Heritage Talking Dictionary*. Copyright © 1997. The Learning Company, Inc. All Rights Reserved.
2. See Avery Dulles, *Models of the Church*, Expanded Edition (New York: Doubleday Image Books, 1987).
3. G. K. Chesterton. *The Thing: Why I Am a Catholic* (New York: Dodd, Mead and Co., 1946), 167.
4. Ronda DeSola Chervin. *Quotable Saints* (Ann Arbor, MI: Servant Publications, 1992), 75.
5. This quotation is from the translation by Henry Wadsworth Longfellow, available on the Internet at http://www.catholic_pages.com/dir/link.asp?ref=21652.
6. John Deedy. *A Book of Catholic Anecdotes* (Allen, TX: Thomas More Publications, 1997), 99.

Chapter Four

1. For a compilation of *Peanuts* strips with religious themes, see Charles M. Schulz, *And the Beagles and the Bunnies Shall Lie Down Together: The Theology in Peanuts* (New York: Holt, Rinehart, Winston, 1984).
2. According to scholarly consensus, Hebrews is not a letter at all but closer to being a homily or theological tract.
3. Jill Haak Adels. *The Wisdom of the Saints: An Anthology* (New York: Oxford University Press, 1987), 49.

Chapter Five
1. Robert Clark. *Mr. White's Confession* (New York: Picador, 1998).
2. Ibid., 341.
3. Clyde Edgerton. *Walking Across Egypt* (New York: Ballantine, 1987, 1988).
4. See *The Seven Mountains of Thomas Merton*, by Michael Mott (Boston: Houghton Mifflin, 1984).
5. Thomas Merton. *New Seeds of Contemplation* (New York: New Directions, 1961), 130.
6. Thomas Merton. *A Witness to Freedom: Letters in Times of Crisis*, selected and edited by William H. Shannon (New York: Farrar, Straus & Giroux, 1994).
7. Personal recollection of the author.
8. Leonard Maltin. *Leonard Maltin's 1999 Movie & Video Guide* (New York: Signet Books, 1999), 1433.
9. *Catechism of the Catholic Church*, Second edition, n. 2796.
10. Both quotations are from George J. Marlin, et al., *The Quotable Chesterton* (San Francisco: Ignatius Press, 1986), 122.
11. Quoted in Teresa de Bertadano, *The Book of Catholic Wisdom: 2000 Years of Spiritual Writing* (Chicago: Loyola Press, 2001), 195.

Chapter Six
1. Thomas à Kempis. *The Imitation of Christ*. Edited and translated by Joseph N. Tylenda, S.J. (New York: Vintage Spiritual Classics, 1998), 111.
2. Ibid., 3–4.
3. *The Cloud of Unknowing*, edited and with an Introduction by William Johnston (New York: Doubleday Image Books, 1973), 115–116.
4. *The Little Flowers of St. Francis*, translated by E. M. Blaiklock and A. C. Keyes (Ann Arbor, MI: Servant Publications, 1985).
5. Ibid., 59.
6. Ibid., 60.
7. Ibid., 60.
8. Ibid., 60.
9. Ibid., 61–62.

Chapter Seven

1. Dorothy Day. *The Long Loneliness* (San Francisco: HarperSanFrancisco, 1952), 284.
2. Mary Ann Fatula, O.P. "Faith," in *The New Dictionary of Catholic Spirituality*, Michael Downey, ed. (Collegeville, MN: The Liturgical Press, 1993), 381.
3. See Canon 751: ". . .apostasy is the total repudiation of the Christian faith . . ."
4. Caryll Houselander. *This War is the Passion* (New York: Sheed & Ward, 1941). Quoted in Teresa de Bertodano, ed., *The Book of Catholic Wisdom* (Chicago: Loyola Press, 2001), 220.
5. Thomas Merton. *Conjectures of a Guilty Bystander* (New York: Doubleday Image Books, 1966, 1968), 89.

Chapter Eight

1. Karl Rahner. "Death," in Karl Rahner, ed., *Encyclopedia of Theology: The Concise* Sacramentum Mundi (New York: The Seabury Press, 1975), 332.
2. Ibid., 333.
3. Ibid., 333.
4. Thomas Lynch. *Bodies in Motion and at Rest* (New York: W.W. Norton & Co., 2000), 91.
5. Thomas Merton. *The Wisdom of the Desert* (New York: New Directions, 1960), 63.
6. Quoted in Maisie Ward, *Caryll Houselander: That Divine Eccentric* (Westminster, MD: Christian Classics, Inc., 1988), 307.

Chapter Nine

1. For an articulate defense of biblical fundamentalism, see Harold Lindsell, *The Battle for the Bible* (Grand Rapids, MI: Zondervan, 1976).
2. *Catechism of the Catholic Church*, Second edition, Glossary.
3. Thomas Merton. *New Seeds of Contemplation* (New York: New Directions, 1961), 134–135.
4. *Catechism of the Catholic Church*, Second edition, n. 1.
5. Gerald O'Collins, S.J., and Edward G. Farrugia, S.J. *A Concise Dictionary of Theology*, Revised and Expanded Edition (Mahwah, NJ: Paulist Press, 2000), 121.

6. See Exodus 20:2–17 and Deuteronomy 5:6–21.
7. See Mitch Finley, *The Ten Commandments: Timeless Challenges for Today* (Liguori, MO: Liguori Publications, 2000).
8. *Catechism of the Catholic Church*, Second Edition, n. 40 and 42. The *Catechism* indicates in a footnote that the quotation is from the "*Liturgy of St. John Chrysostom*, Anaphora."
9. See Robert A. Krieg, "Apostles' Creed," in Richard P. McBrien, general editor, *The HarperCollins Encyclopedia of Catholicism* (San Francisco: HarperSanFrancisco, 1995), 75.
10. Ibid., 75.

Chapter Ten
1. Gerald O'Collins, S.J., and Edward G. Farrugia, S.J. *A Concise Dictionary of Theology*, Revised and Expanded Edition (Mahwah, NJ: Paulist Press, 2000), 67.
2. Saint Thomas Aquinas. *Summa Theologiae: A Concise Translation*, edited by Thomas McDermott (Westminster, MD: Christian Classics, 1989), 331.
3. *The Cloud of Unknowing.* William Johnston, trans. New York: Image Books, 1968), 32.
4. Thomas Merton. *New Seeds of Contemplation* (New York: New Directions, 1961), 126–127.
5. Mary Ann Fatula, O.P. "Faith," in Michael Downey, ed., *The New Dictionary of Catholic Spirituality* (Collegeville, MN: The Liturgical Press, 1993), 387.

Afterword
1. Gerald O'Collins, S.J., and Edward G. Farrugia, S.J. *A Concise Dictionary of Theology*, Revised and Expanded Edition (Mahwah, NJ: Paulist Press, 2000), 86.
2. Ibid., 86.
3. *Desert Wisdom: Sayings From the Desert Fathers*, trans. by Yushi Nomura (Maryknoll, NY: Orbis Books, 2001), 3.